THE LAST FRONTIERS ON EARTH
Strange Places Where You Can Live Free
BY JON FISHER

THE LAST FRONTIERS ON EARTH
Strange Places Where You Can Live Free
© *1980, 1985 by Loompanics Unlimited*

Dedication
To RAYO, who walked this trail before any of us thought of it.

PUBLISHED BY:
Loompanics Unlimited
PO Box 1197
Port Townsend, WA 98368
U.S.A.

ISBN 0-915179-24-5
Library Of Congress Catalog Card Number 84-52484

TABLE OF CONTENTS

INTRODUCTION

*"But man's capacities have never been measured; nor are
we to judge of what he can do by any precedents, so little
has been tried.*
    -Henry David Thoreau

Are you fed up with taxes that go nowhere but up and up? Have you had it with the snoopy government that keeps digging always deeper into your private affairs and is forever telling you that you can't do this and that you have to do that? Is your boss a pain in the ass? Is the noise and pollution and traffic of the city driving your up a wall? Wouldn't you like to get away to some place where people would just leave you alone so you could live your own life and do as you please? Well, maybe this is the solution to your problems.

For several centuries, up to a few decades ago, anyone living in North America who felt confined and oppressed by the civilization, the government, the social rules, or the taxes and tithes demanded of him in the built up, settled areas could easily escape all that by moving west to the frontier. With the coming of the twentieth century, the frontier as it was formerly understood has disappeared on this continent. Now, just when government is more intrusive and demanding than ever, and constantly getting worse, the ready escape route seems to be closed. Some freedom seekers look to outer space as the only hope to find a place where people can be free again on a new wide open frontier. But it's far too soon to give up on Old Mother Earth. With enough imagination and some redefining of the idea of "frontier", we can find numerous places and niches that are waiting to be put to use by adventurous people who insist on being free.

When they think about frontiers, most people assume that all the suitable places on Earth have already been settled. All that's left are some barren areas where no one could possibly live, they think. This is much too pessimistic. Antarctica alone consists of 5½ million empty square miles. The empty oceans cover 70% of the Earth's surface and add up to about 141 million square miles. How's that for a little elbow room?

But the skeptic will reply: "Sure, but people can't live in those places in the familiar, comfortable way we live in the temperate land areas on Earth". What the skeptic forgets is that humans are tropical animals by nature. We couldn't live in the temperate zones either without certain technology, namely clothing, fire, and artificial shelters. It was the invention of this technology that opened up the frontiers of the temperate zones to us tropical animals.

What we see happening now is that just recently, in the last hundred years or so, we have begun developing the technology that will allow us to inhabit these new frontiers of the oceans and polar regions. Sure, the pioneers into these new areas will find the conditions strange and difficult. But imagine what the northern winter must have seemed like to the first humans who experienced it. In a few generations, or maybe sooner, life in these new frontiers will seem as familiar and ordinary as life now seems in the settled areas of populous countries. Future ocean and polar dwellers will find it amusing to think that anyone ever questioned whether humans could live in such a place.

The following chapters may be considered an exercise in speculative geography. This begins with descriptive geography, an accurate describing of the conditions existing in various exotic places; and goes on from there into speculation about how these places might be used and inhabited by people who want to get away from all existing societies. Some chapters describe ways of life that may be pursued while physically staying within presently inhabited places, ways of life that create free spaces, new frontiers, within existing societies by playing the game by *your* rules rather than theirs.

Every chapter following discusses a way to live, sometimes with several variations, that would allow you to be totally free of any existing government if you so choose. Anyone who truly wants to be free to live his life as he chooses doesn't need to be told why this is desirable. Governments, totalitarians, bureaucrats, socialists, and fascists have hunted down and stamped out freedom in all settled places. These authoritarians apparently won't be satisfied until everyone is taxed to the limit that they can endure and bound down with regulations until every act is either prohibited or mandatory. The rule-makers net covers a wide area, all ordinary land on Earth is claimed by some government -- but even so, there remain many places on Earth that still lie beyond their reach, as the following chapters will reveal.

Everything worthwhile has its price. You can have as much

freedom as you want, if you are willing to pay the price to get it. Frontiersmen always have to leave certain comforts and advantages of civilization behind them. Most people don't have the guts to leave their cozy nests even if they are ruled by an iron-fisted tyrant. The following chapters will explore the costs of achieving freedom in various ways and places. You can decide whether the prize is worth the price in your own situation.

A few general comments are in order concerning the ideas expressed in the following chapters: These ideas are meant to be mind-expanding suggestions, not definitive, not the last word. These chapters contain only the briefest sketches of the lifeways presented. Use them to inspire further such concepts or variations on these ideas. Feel free to change things around in your mind, add details, embellish and embroider them, and work into them elements of your own fondest hopes and dreams. In all cases further research will be required before you take action, and some sources of additional information are mentioned at the end of each chapter.

Note that the ways of life suggested in many cases need not require a life-long committment. One could live in some of these ways for a couple of years and then move on to something else. Also keep in mind the possibility of combining ideas that are presented in different chapters. For example, one could live as a foot nomad while travelling between hideouts located in several ghost towns, or one could combine life aboard an airship with extended visits to several uninhabited islands. Keep your mind open to other creative combinations like these which may better suit your own desires.

Some of these ideas have already been put into practice by people who are now living the ways of life described. So there can be no doubt that such existing lifeways are possible. other ideas are only speculation at this time and await the daring pioneer who will be the first to actually undertake such a life. Those whose desire for freedom is only lukewarm and not a consuming inferno, the timid, the complacent, and any who are not willing to consider basic changes in their way of life, will not find a solution to their problems in these pages. But if you have what it takes to be a trail-blazing pioneer, perhaps you will find what you need in one of these last frontiers on Earth.

PART I
LIVE IN THE POLAR REGIONS

CHAPTER 1
LIVE IN ANTARCTICA

Antarctica is the largest uninhabited area on Earth, 5½ million square miles, larger than the United States and Mexico combined, with no permanent population. About 800 people overwinter in all of Antarctica, and the number swells to 2,000 or so in summer, but only two women have ever stayed there through a winter. Ordinary settlements of families are not yet found south of the Falkland Islands (which have a population of a little over 2,000) except for a small settlement, Grytviken, on South Georgia. Of the 40 or so stations in the Antarctic regions, only Stanley, Falkland Islands is larger than a small hamlet.

The largest station on the Antarctic continent itself is the US McMurdo Station on Ross Island which has a population of about 200 in winter and up to 1,000 in summer. The station has facilities similar to what you'd expect in any small hamlet. It has a sprawling appearance somewhat like a mining town, with streets, housing facilities, a harbor, a fire station, community center, shops, a church, and a hospital. Since the year to year snow accumulation isn't a problem, most buildings rest on the ground surface and appear rather conventional. Electricity for McMurdo was supplied by a nuclear power plant from 1962 until 1972. But the nuclear station has since been dismantled, and electric power is now produced by diesel generators. Drinking water is made from sea water in a desalination plant.

Most of Antarctica (98%) is covered by the world's largest ice sheet, but this still leaves about 200,000 square miles of the continent ice-free in summer. However, even in the ice-free regions, the ground is frozen to a depth of 1,000 feet in permafrost. The thickness of the ice cap ranges up to 15,000 feet. Most of the top surface of the ice lies between 6,500 feet to 13,000 feet above sea level, with some mountain peaks rising to more than 16,000 feet. This means that Antarctica has an average altitude nearly three times higher than any other continent. This altitude accounts in part for the extreme cold of interior Antarctica, which is much colder than similar Arctic latitides. From the interior of Antarctica, the ice sheet flows outward in all directions to the ocean. Along almost half of the coast, the ice feeds into ice shelves, which comprise more than

10% of the continent's area. The shelves are floating sheets of continental ice with level or rolling surfaces and thicknesses of 650 to 4,000 feet. The three largest ice shelves are the Ross, the Ronne, and Amery; the Ross Ice Shelf alone is larger than France! These ice shelves move seaward at speeds of 3,000 to 4,000 feet per year, and tabular icebergs calf off of their seaward edges.

There is hardly any plant life in Antarctica; mosses and lichens make up most of what little there is. And there are no land animals. Along the coasts one finds seals, penguins, and sea birds that live off the sea. But in most of the interior there is no life at all -- no plants, no animals, not even bacteria.

Until recently, Antarctica's only value was for scientific research. But evidence is now available which indicates that this frozen wasteland conceals a bonanza of untapped resources. Researchers have found large quantities of coal, and there are indications of perhaps large fields of oil and natural gas offshore. Some of the other minerals that have been found include gold, platinum, iron, copper, nickel, cobalt and uranium. The sea surrounding Antarctica teems with tiny marine life called krill which could become a major source of protein in world markets. So the economic base for an extractive economy appears to exist in Antarctica. Fortunes could probably be made extracting and shipping out the mineral and energy resources, if the transportation problems could be solved. And the energy resources are there which would make self-sustaining comm- unities possible on the continent.

Other advantages that an Antarctic settlement would enjoy are that it would have an unlimited supply of fresh water available in the ice and snow. And, away from the few existing stations, Antarctica is one of the least polluted places on Earth. There is a garbage problem near the present research stations, in part due to the fact that organic wastes will never decompose there due to the frigid temperatures. But an independent settlement that didn't receive government support would want to practice maximum recycling of its material resources anyway for economic reasons, and this would go a long way toward solving the refuse problem.

But many problems stand in the way of large scale civilized development of Antarctica. There is a lack of permanent

MAP # 1:

Known Mineral Occurences In Antarctica

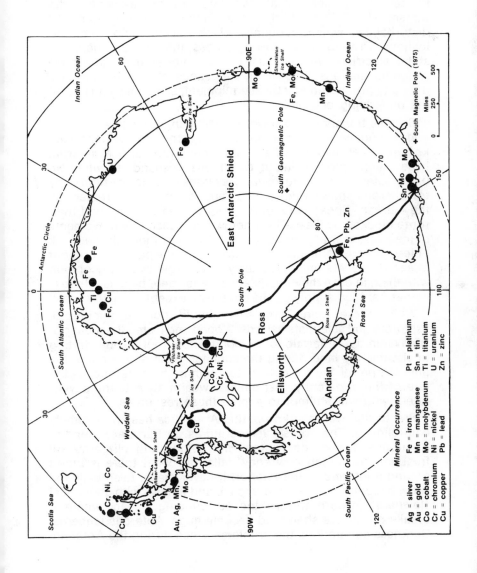

harbors, and sea transport is tricky due to the varying conditions of the sea ice. Airfields are few and widely scattered. Communications can sometimes be difficult in Antarctica due to certain problems that can interfere greatly with radio transmissions. There is the aurora accompanied by electrical disturbances which frequently black out all radio communications. Drifting snow blowing across antennas can generate static electricity which causes radio interference. And those Antarctic stations that sit on thousands of feet of ice have difficulty grounding electrical equipment, since they can't get at the underlying bedrock.

Surface transport and travel are still dangerous in Antarctica and it is not wise for a person to travel alone. People have been known to get disoriented and lost only a few yards away from base camp when whiteout conditions descend, or when an unexpected blizzard blows up. Crevasses that may be hidden by treacherous snow bridges are a serious hazard to travellers on the ice cap. Those who journey on the sea ice may find their route blocked by "leads" of open water, caused by movements of ice floes, that appear suddenly in front of them, or the block of ice they are riding may break away from the pack and drift out to sea. Travellers must also carry an emergency supply of food with them in case they get delayed somewhere because there is no natural food supply on the continent, except along the coast.

While these many problems should not be minimized, explorers and scientists have developed and tested the means of survival in the Antarctic to the point where tourists are starting to vist this icy land during the summer. So it appears that the time is ripe for the next phase to begin in the Antarctic, as the lure of the apparently vast mineral wealth attracts the adventurers who will attempt to exploit these resources.

Practically everyone knows that Antarctica has an extremely cold climate. The coldest temperatures on Earth are found in Antarctica during the winter. High winds and blizzards are frequent. Not much new snow falls, but what there is blows around a lot, and in the interior, it never melts. Eventually the snow becomes compressed into ice and it flows with geological slowness outward toward the surrounding ocean, where it breaks off the ice shelves to become huge, Antarctic icebergs. Darkness compounds the problems, since during the Antarctic winter the sun doesn't rise above the horizon for up to 6 months. During the summer, near the coast, the temperature may rise to a little above freezing. Some lake beds fill with a shallow depth of meltwater. Some hardy plants manage to grow and blossom and bear seeds. During these summer months the sun shines around the clock. Because of the sunshine, there are times when it doesn't seem as cold as the temperature would indicate. Sunbathing bare to the waist can be a pleasant experience under the Antarctic summer sun, even when the temperature is below freezing, provided there is no wind blowing. But the slightest breeze will send the daring sunbather running for cover. It would seem that a glassed-in sun room would be a pleasant place to spend time during the Antarctic summer. And food plants could be readily grown within such an enclosure.

Despite this rigorous climate, the heroic age of Antarctic exploration ended long ago. While Antarctica is no place for the foolhardy, living there is no more dangerous for one who is properly prepared and who uses good common sense than for example, working in a steel mill is. Scientists and explorers have developed shelter and clothing and vehicles and techniques fully able to cope with the harsh conditions.

Antarctic buildings whose foundations rest on rock are not much different from structures found in any cold climate. They must, of course, be well sealed and insulated. But desireable bare rock building sites are scarce in Antarctica. Many stations are located on the ice cap,thousands of feet above bedrock. And building on ice presents a special problem.

At Byrd Station it was found that, over the years, the escaping heat tended to melt the ice under the buildings, causing the buildings to sink into the ice. Meanwhile, the snow piled up on top, compounding the problem. Digging down to clear the doors and windows became an increasingly difficult chore. Finally, the old Byrd Station had to be abandoned and New Byrd was build nearby using a different plan.

The construction of New Byrd Station began with the gouging out of huge trenches in the ice, large enough so that entire buildings could be assembled down inside them. These structures were built on platforms raised up off the ice to minimize loss of heat through conduction and melting of the ice below. Then the trenches were covered over with arches and the snow was allowed to accumulate on top. The closed-in space inside the trenches is lighted, but it is kept cold so that the ice won't melt. This technique appears to have solved the problem of sinking buildings. It gives the inhabitants of New Byrd double protection against the harsh Antarctic weather. And it provides them with an "out of doors" space inside the trenches which is cold, but is protected from the wind and from the blizzards that may be raging up on top.

In addition, those intent on living free will see at once how well concealed New Byrd is. If a company of freedom-seeking settlers were to build a station somewhere on the millions of square miles of the mostly uninhabited Antarctic ice cap, using the cut-and-cover technique developed at New Byrd, they would have achieved almost perfect concealment from unwanted visitors.

Such a free settlement would find itself in an unusually favorable position in regard to government sovereignty. Seven nations claim parts of Antarctica: Argentina, Australia, Chile, France, New Zealand, Norway, and the United Kingdom. Most of these claims slice the continent into pie-shaped wedges that converge at the South Pole, and the claims of Chile, Argentina, and the UK overlap across the Antarctic Peninsula. But these claims do not restrict current activities since they have been suspended for the duration of the Antarctic Treaty that is presently in force.

Neither the US nor the USSR has made any claims to Antarctic territory and neither recognizes any that have been made. The US pointedly has not claimed the sector (Marie Byrd Land) that was left for it by the other claimants. But both the US and the Soviets have been conducting extensive research in Antarctica in recent years. Soviet bases are located mainly in the sector claimed by Austalia, but activities during the time the Antarctic Treaty is in force are not supposed to form any basis for later territorial claims.

"Effective occupation" is the only one of the reasons for ownership advanced by the Antarctic claimants that is recognized by international law and, until recently, there has been none on the continent. Discovery sometimes has been moot because explorers could not tell ice or cloud banks from land.

International law views the hoisting of flags, dropping of written claims, nailing of plaques and other token acts as only "fictitious occupation". Nor has the sector principle itself any legal basis or relation to Antarctic reality. So the question of government sovereignty in Antarctica is at best unclear.

Furthermore, despite the various territorial claims, the basic law governing Antarctica at present is the Antarctic Treaty, signed by twelve nations in 1959. Under the Treaty, all land and sea area south of 60 degrees of latitude is reserved for peaceful scientific pursuits. All military activity is prohibited, and the various conflicting territorial claims are suspended for 30 years (until 1989). This means that no government owns any of the land in Antarctica. This situation may change after 1989 when various national claims may be reasserted, or the Treaty may be extended. However, at present each signatory to the Treaty has jurisdiction over its own citizens wherever they may be in Antarctica, but no government has jurisdiction over territory. Since all stations now in Antarctica are operated by some government or other, this policy works without many problems. But I wonder what would happen if a private, non-government group of settlers were to set up a station in Antarctica. It would be especially interesting if those settlers happened to be citizens of a country which was not a signatory of the Treaty. It happens that most nations have not signed the Treaty. The only ones that have signed it are nations that have sent researchers to the Antarctic.

Suppose a party made up of citizens of some non-signatory nation, say Liberia or El Salvador, for example, were to establish a settlement in Antarctica. It appears that, under the Treaty, no government would have sovereignty over them. Of course, such a free settlement shouldn't rely too much on this legal fine point for their protection. Governments ultimately depend on raw power and they have a habit of "interpreting" even the most plain language in any perverse way that happens to further their interests. Still the Treaty does give a free settlement a solid legal leg to stand on, which may be combined with the de facto reality of their existence, and their concealment under the ice, and a determined defense, and the extremely strong natural defenses resulting from the harsh climate and barely passable terrain, and the unattractive nature of the prize to be won; put all these factors together and you see that Antarctica offers one of the best places on Earth to establish a politically free and independent community, a refuge for persons with a powerful desire to live free.

For more information, see:

THE ANTARCTIC by H.G.R. King, Arco, New York, 1969. *A thorough discussion of the physical conditions, geography and history of the Antarctic region.*

"World's Last Frontier Heating Up: Global Race For Antarctica's Riches," US NEWS AND WORLD REPORT, February 28, 1977.

POLAR REGIONS ATLAS, by the CIA. 1978, Superintendent of Documents, US Goverment Printing Office, Washington, DC 20402, stock number 041-015-00094-2. *An excellent detailed survey of the Antarctic (and the Arctic) with dozens of maps.*

WINTER HIKING AND CAMPING, by John A. Danielson. Adirondack Mountain Club, Glen Falls, New York, 1972. *This is relevant to Antarctica because it covers the human body's response to cold, clothing, equipment, first aid, survival and rescue under frigid conditions.*

OCEANS (magazine). Publication of the Oceanic Society, 6 issues per year, membership $15.00 per year. *Number 3, 1977 issue is entirely about Antarctica.* Oceanic Society, PO Box 10167, Des Moines, IA 50340.

CHAPTER 2

LIVE ON THE ARCTIC ICECAP

In 1893, Fridtjof Nansen embarked on an expedition that he hoped would make him the first man to reach the north pole. In 1884 he had read that some wreckage of the ship "Jeannette", which had been crushed by the ice off the north coast of Siberia, had been found embedded in ice washed ashore in southwest Greenland. Nansen realized that this movement of debris from Siberia to Greenland meant that an ice floe had drifted across the Arctic, possible right over the pole. An explorer, he thought, could also ride on that drift, and thus perhaps reach the pole.

Nansen's plan was to build a small, sturdy ship that could withstand being frozen into the ice. The sides of the ship should be rounded, he thought, with a sufficient slope to keep the ice from getting a firm hold on the hull. Then the pressure of the ice would lift the ship right up out of the water. It took him several years to raise the money for his expedition, but at last he was able to build his ship, which he named the "Fram".

The "Fram" was outfitted with sails and coal burning auxiliary engines. Nansen laid in provisions for five years, took 12 men along with him, and sailed from his native Norway for the Arctic on June 24, 1893. The expedition headed north then east around the coast of Norway and along the Siberian coast to a point near where the "Jeannette" had been lost. Then they headed due north, and by September the "Fram" was locked in the ice.

At first, all went well. As the ice closed in and squeezed the ship, it resisted the pressure and rose up undamaged as it had been designed to do. The drift of the ice began carrying them northward toward their goal. But then the direction of the drift began shifting more and more westward, until they were making no more northern headway at all. It became apparent that the "Fram" would not reach more than 84 degrees latitide. It would pass some 350 miles short of the north pole.

Nansen couldn't let the prize slip away without making one last daring attempt at it. He hastily planned a secondary expedition to consist of himself and one companion who would take sledges and dogs and make a dash over the ice for the pole. Leaving the "Fram" under the command of Captain Sverdrup, Nansen set out for the pole on March 14, 1895, taking with him

Hjalmar Johansen, 3 sledges and 28 dogs. In just under a month they had reached 86° 14′ north, closer to the pole than anyone had penetrated up to that time.

But time was running out. The condition of the ice had become very bad, impeding forward progress. To the north all they could see was an almost impassible chaos of iceblocks and soon, they knew, the summer breakup of ice would begin. There was no chance of finding the "Fram" again, and the nearest land was 400 miles to the southwest. So reluctantly they turned around and headed back. After 130 days they reached Franz Joseph Land.

Nansen's return journey was a great adventure filled with many hardships. But that is not our main concern here. Our eyes turn mainly to Nansen's ship. The "Fram" continued on drifting with the ice for a total of 35 months until it broke free northwest of Spitzbergen. Undamaged, it sailed back to Norway, arriving home on August 20, 1896, to find Nansen waiting on the dock to greet them. Nansen's expedition was a great success, even though he didn't quite get to the north pole. the data gathered greatly advanced man's knowledge of the polar ocean. And not one man was lost.

What is of greatest interest to us is that Nansen demonstrated one way that men can live on the Arctic Ocean. Once men have lived in a place for three years, and come out none the worse for it, there is no longer any question whether survival is possible in such a place. The prospect of living there then becomes a question of economics. Following Nansen's lead, a company of hardy souls could build a ship along the lines of the "Fram" (which, by the way, may still be seen in a museum in Norway). Modern materials and engineering would make possible great improvements in design over what Nansen could do in the 1890's. These pioneers would sail their ship into the Arctic Ocean, until their arctic home became locked in the ice with which it would drift just as the "Fram" did long ago.

How would such polar settlers live? The Arctic Ocean is not rich in resources, in fact the polar regions have been called deserts. About the only sources of food one might find on the arctic icecap are some seals and polar bears, and they are quite rare. Arctic settlers would have to raise their own food. Transport to a settlement locked in the ice would not be easy.

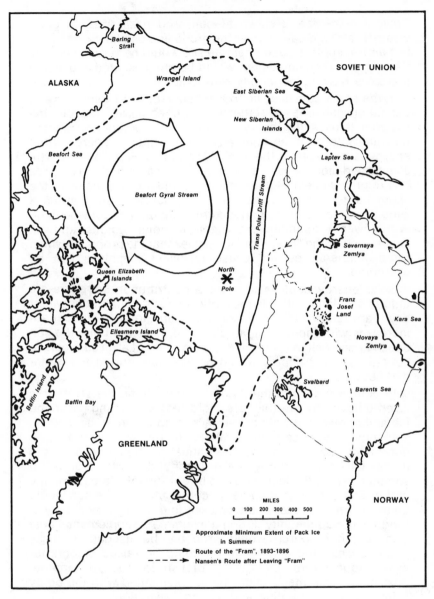

Travel on the ice is slow, difficult, and hazardous. In good weather, a plane can fly over the arctic and can land on the ice, but air transport to such a remote site would be very expensive. Clearly, an arctic settlement would be quite isolated and would therefore have to be largely self-sufficient.

In the end it comes down to a question of energy sources and capital investment. A settlement can endlessly recycle the material it uses (in theory) provided it is equipped with the machinery to do it, and has a sufficient input of energy. What energy is available in the arctic? When the "Fram" went north, she carried along a five years' supply of coal to fuel the engines and to provide heat. But the engines could not be used while the "Fram" was locked in the ice, so, in addition, she carried a windmill which powered an electric generator to provide light. Windpower is abundantly available in polar regions, and the experience of the "Fram" demonstrates that the problems which frigid temperatures will cause for wind machines can be overcome.

Solar energy could also make a contribution but there are unique problems with it in the arctic. In northern latitudes winter days are short and summer days are long. This pattern increases with increasing latitude until, near the pole, the sun doesn't rise at all in winter and it doesn't set at all in summer. Of course, no solar energy would be available during the winter darkness.

In summer, despite the 24 hours of daylight, the weather is often unfavorable. In this less frigid season, melting snow and ice and open water hold the surface temperature to near 32° F, sometimes rising as high as 40° F. Rain as well as snow falls during the arctic summer. The annual precipitation of 4 to 6 inches falls mostly during late summer and autumn storms. So summer days with clear skies and bright sunshine are rare in the arctic. Still, although the energy contribution of the sun would be small, greenhouses could be used to grow a year's supply of food for the community during the summer. Supplemental heat from another source would probably be needed in these greenhouses. And small animals could be raised indoors for meat. Aquaculture, the raising of fish for food, is another possibility. This menu might be supplemented with the booty from occasional hunting and fishing expeditions.

A more promising energy source would be an ocean thermal

energy conversion system *(OTEC)*. Open water at the surface of the Arctic Ocean has a temperature of 29° F while the air above it may be -20° F or lower. That's a large 50 degree temperature difference, not even considering the effect of wind chill. To harness this temperature difference, an arctic OTEC would use a working fluid that would boil at a temperature in the 20's. The boiler would be placed in the water down under the ice. Leaving the boiler, the vapor would drive a turbine which would power a generator to produce electricity. Then the vapor would be condensed in coils exposed to the frigid air, and would return again to the boiler in a closed cycle. A plant like this could provide huge amounts of power, especially during the winter when the air is colder and the temperature difference is larger.

Another possibility is that the arctic habitat could be equipped with a nuclear power plant, like that used in many submarines and ships and at McMurdo Station in the Antarctic, which would only have to be refueled at rare intervals.

Or, going back to an older energy source that Nansen used on the "Fram", an arctic drift station could burn coal. This could be conveniently obtained from the coal mines on the arctic island of Svalbard. Either the arctic station could put into Svaldbard every few years to replenish its supply, or coal could be delivered to it via airship (blimp).

Note that oil and gas, although they are abundant in the arctic, could not be conveniently used by a drift station. The problems are that gas is usually delivered by means of a pipeline and you can't run a pipeline to a moving station. The problem with oil is that it is not usually consumed in the crude form, but first has to be refined into various products. And there are no convenient oil refineries in the arctic.

There are a couple other ways that a group might live on the Arctic Ocean. The US nuclear submarine "Nautilus" made the first crossing of the arctic via the North Pole under the ice in 1958. Since then, nuclear subs routinely cruise under the polar ice. Conceivably, a submarine could be outfitted as a permanent habitation for a community. Such a vessel could stay under the ice (or travel anywhere in the world ocean). Nuclear power is really the only feasible energy source for such a vessel. It could not readily exploit the wind, solar, or sea thermal energy available in the arctic. And it could rise to the surface only through those occasional "leads" of open water that it could find, unless it was able to melt through the typically 13 feet or more of the normal pack ice. Still, such a submarine habitat would be completely protected from storms on the surface, and it would certainly be well concealed from anyone who would do it harm.

Another formation, found in the arctic, that would be suitable for a permanent settlement is the ice island. It is not feasible to build permanent structures on the ordinary pack ice because it is in constant motion, breaking up and refreezing. An ordinary ice floe may stay in one piece for a couple of years. But the action of wind and currents and storms may just as likely crack it in half or break it up into little pieces at any time. But an ice island is quite different.

The US Air Force found the first known ice island in 1946. They could see rocks and streams on it and thought that it was land, although it was located where no land was supposed to be. Then they discovered that it was moving and realized its true nature.

These ice islands begin as land ice that flows down into the Ellesmere Island Ice Shelf. Occasionally, large, flat sections break away from the northern edge of the ice shelf and join the moving pack. These ice islands may be up to 20 miles wide, hundreds of square miles in area, and 200 feet thick, compared to the 13 foot average thickness of the sea ice. They float slowly in erratic clockwise circles around the North American side of the Arctic Ocean and eventually exit to the Atlantic, where they melt in the warmer water. Many have been observed for as long as 30 years. Most ice islands in the arctic are small; of the more than 100 tabular fragments recorded, only seven have been large enough to accomodate manned research stations. These ice islands make ideal bases for permanent settlements in the arctic because they are extremely durable. They don't break up like ordinary ice floes -- in fact, they plow through ordinary sea ice like a bulldozer through a sand pile.

Ice islands are at the mercy of the currents, however. One ice island, Arlis II, floated down into the North Atlantic east of Greenland. The scientists who were living on it had to be airlifted off, as the island underneath their permanent buildings melted away. But as long as an ice island stays within the Arctic Ocean, it doesn't melt. It remains as a permanent feature, drifting around with the current.

An ice island would make an excellent base on which a party of freedom seekers might establish a settlement. The only natural threat to such a settlement would be that their island might drift out of the Arctic Ocean to a warmer latitude where it would melt. But the chances of finding an undiscovered ice island are slim. The US Air Force flies regular reconaissance flights over the arctic. And the military forces of other nations probably also fly such patrols. They would be the ones most likely to find any ice islands that remain unknown. Of course, a known island like T-3, which has a US ice station on it, is plenty big enough for another settlement to be established on it, in addition to the one already there. But, while it is not clear whether the US government actually claims this island as its property, still, another settlement could not be established there without at least tacit approval of US authorities. I think a party of freedom seekers would find such a location to be too much under the eye of the US military to be comfortable with it. So it seems that the best approach to living on the Arctic Ocean is to use a ship designed along the lines of Nansen's "Fram".

It must be admitted that the weather in the polar regions is among the worst in the world. Why would anyone want to live in such an unpleasant place? Well, let's take a look at some of the advantages. Legally, living in an arctic station would be much like living aboard a boat in international waters. You would be effectively out from under the authority of any government. To strengthen your legal position, you would want to register your vessel with some small "flag of convenience" nation like Liberia. An arctic station would be quite secluded. As of 1966, only 3 small ice stations were to be found in all the 2½ million square miles of the Arctic Ocean. Storms would be less of a problem on the pack ice than on the open ocean to the south, since there are no towering waves or turbulent seas to toss a ship around or capsize it. It's true that the ice does move, but only slowly by comparison. And the ice does exert tremendous pressure, but, like the "Fram," a vessel can be built to withstand such forces and to rise up over the ice rather than be crushed by it. The artic region, in addition, offers an almost untouched environment, as free from pollution as any place on Earth. And unlimited drinking water can be obtained by melting snow and old weathered ice.

An arctic abode would rate very high in security. There is no local population, and the virtually impassible terrain would prevent any private aggressors coming in from outside. Only a government could afford the expense of sending a military force into this region. And a small, peaceful arctic station would probably not be enough of a prize to arouse any government to take such action. One exception is the Soviet Union, which might perceive a station that drifted too close to Siberia as a threat to its security.

One factor that would enhance the security of an arctic station is the ease of concealment. Fliers who have attempted to find parties on the ice testify to the incredible difficulty of finding anything in that vast white wilderness. If arctic settlers let their station accumulate ice and snow and tried to hide it rather than reveal it, it would be very difficult indeed for an outsider to find.

An arctic station on the surface could not use mobility for protection inasmuch as its drift could not be controlled. But the prevailing currents happen to be favorable to a free arctic drift station. There are two main arctic currents: the Transpolar Drift Stream which crosses the USSR side of the Ocean from the New Siberian Islands to the east coast of Greenland, and the Beaufort Gyral Stream which flows in a circle in theBeaufort Sea between Alaska and the North Pole. Nansen's "Fram" drifted on the Transpolar Drift Stream. But a floating arctic station inhabited by freedom seekers would want to position itself within the Beaufort Gyral Stream where it would tend to go round and round on the North American side of the Arctic Ocean, and it would not get into waters of interest to the Russians.

Like any other ocean, the Arctic is international water, outside the jurisdiction of any government. However, the Soviets have made various sweeping claims to their side of the Ocean. These claims have not been recognized by any other government, nor have they been enforced or even pressed very strongly by the Soviets. Still, it would be prudent for a free arctic station to stay away from the Soviet side, and they could conveniently do this by positioning themselves within the Beaufort Gyral Stream.

Like a small boat, an arctic station would have limited living space. But, in favorable weather, the pack ice itself could be used for various activities, so arctic settlers wouldn't be as cooped up as people living aboard a ship sailing on a warmer ocean.

The cost of setting up an arctic station would definitely be in the high range. One possible way to defray some of that cost would be to establish the station, at least in part, as a scientific station. This might also provide some income to some of the residents in payment for performing certain scientific chores. A private, non-profit organization with a name like "Institute For Arctic Research" could be set up to build and own and operate the station. Cultivating this image of a peaceful, scientific endeavor would probably minimize political and legal problems. Besides arctic research, another legitimate area of research that the station could pursue is the development of a closed, fully recycling ecosystem. Such research is a necessary prerequisite to the development of space colonies. An arctic station is an ideal place to conduct such research inasmuch as it would have to be as self-sufficient as possible anyway in order to minimize outside subsidy. The only other income opportunities at a small arctic habitat would be those occupations that are independent of location, such as writing, or those which lead to the export of a small, light and valuable product, like artwork. Transportation to and from an arctic station could only be via small aircraft and would be expensive. On the other hand, communication to the outside world via radio would not be difficult, but conversations could be overheard by anyone with adequate radio gear. However, confidentiality could be maintained through the use of a private code.

There are no mineral resources on the ice pack itself. Oil and natural gas may be found under the Ocean, but a small arctic station wouldn't be able to exploit these resources. However, the exploration and drilling now being done in the arctic by oil companies might provide jobs for some of the residents of an arctic settlement.

Talk of living on the arctic ice probably conjures up the image of Eskimoes huddling in an igloo, or of explorers wrapped in bulky parkas, shivering in a tent while a blizzard rages outside. Actually, arctic living does not necessarily imply such a primitive lifestyle. All it takes is capital equipment and a source of energy and even the most luxurious standard of living one

27

might desire could be built in the arctic. Arctic settlers would find that their environment prevents them from doing certain things outside, but that is true of any environment. For example, South Pacific islanders find their environment prohibits their enjoying skiing and tobaganing, which arctic settlers could indulge in amply. Within their constructed habitat, arctic pioneers could develop any lifestyle they want, up to the limit of what their finances would permit.

For more information, see:

TO THE TOP OF THE WORLD, by Charles Kuralt. Holt, Rinehart and Winston, New York, 1968. *An entertaining, highly readable account of the Plaisted Polar Expedition which attempted to reach the North Pole in 1967 on snowmobiles. It contains much detailed information about conditions in the arctic.*

THE FROZEN WORLD, by Thayer Willis, which is Part I of "The Last Frontiers." Doubleday, Garden City, 1971. *Contains a chapter recounting the experiences of Nansen's drift of 1893 to 1896. Other chapters tell about a number of other arctic expeditions.*

POLAR REGIONS ATLAS, by the CIA. 1978, Superintendent of Documents, US Government Printing Office, Washington, DC 20402, stock number 041-015-00094-2. *An excellent detailed survey of the Arctic (and the Antarctic) with dozens of maps.*

COLD WEATHER CAMPING, by Richard Stebbins. Henry Regnery, Chicago, 1976. *Contains information on living with cold weather, which is pertinent to Arctic conditions.*

CHAPTER 3
LIVE ON A FLOATING ICEBERG

Virtually all the land in the world, even the most insignificant pieces of real estate, is owned by some government or other. But vast acreages of habitable "land" are floating around unclaimed by any government. It's not really land, of course, but ice; specifically flat-topped Antarctic icebergs.

Antarctic ice islands, commonly called tabular icebergs, are significantly larger and more numerous than their Arctic counterparts; some with observed horizontal dimensions of more than 35 miles by 60 miles have calved away from the Ross, Ronne and other ice shelves. These huge tabular floes, towering as high as 250 feet or more above the sea surface, have been observed grounded at depths of 1,600 feet (80% to 90% of the vertical height of an iceberg rides below the surface of the water). Antarctic icebergs rarely find their way into Southern Hemisphere shipping lanes; consequently, no monitoring service has been set up to keep watch on them, such as exists in the North Atlantic. Most Antarctic icebergs drift in a circular course around the Antarctic continent, often for several years before melting and breaking up.

Arctic icebergs, on the other hand, are significantly different. Just about all icebergs found in the North Atlantic have broken away from glaciers rather than from flat ice sheets. As a result, they are jagged and irregular lumps of ice with no flat surfaces. As they melt faster underwater than above, the center of gravity shifts until they roll over in the water suddenly and without warning. These features make Arctic icebergs quite unsuitable for habitation, unlike Antarctic ice islands, which look very attractive in that respect.

So here's the game plan: a freedom seeker could select a suitable iceberg in the Southern Ocean, choosing one from the millions that are available. He could erect his habitat on it, similar to the many ice stations that already exist in the polar regions. The berg could be insulated to retard melting. If the berg was left to drift free, it might last for many years. It wouldn't melt until it happened to drift out of the polar waters into the warmer waters to the north. If the iceberg began to melt seriously, the habitat would be taken off. Then another iceberg could be found and the cycle repeated.

There are two possible variations on this basic plan: One is to make a temporary home on an iceberg while riding it to some dry country where it would be sold as a source of fresh water. (Icebergs originate as snow that has been compacted into ice so they are entirely fresh water ice, not salt water.) Australia, Arabia, and some dry regions in South America are all possible destinations and customers. Australia may be the first goal, since it is closer to the Southern Ocean. Arabia would be a more lucrative market, but it would be harder to get to, since that would require crossing the tropics without unacceptable melting. A journey like this might take one to three years. During the voyage, the iceberg could be registered as a ship, which would clarify its legal status and ownership. After all, ships come in many shapes and sizes, and are made of several different materials: wood, steel, even concrete, so why not a ship made of ice? The iceberg would be moved by towing or pushing it very slowly with powerful tugs, making full use of appropriate ocean currents. At the voyage's end, the habitat would be taken off and transported back to Antarctica, where another berg would be selected so the cycle could be repeated. The sale of the iceberg in a thirsty country would provide a large income. So this could be a profitable operation, provided that expenses could be kept low enough.

Actually, this concept is not an entirely new idea. Many years ago small icebergs were towed from Antarctica to the west coast of South America. This hasn't been done recently, but the trade could be revived. Presently, the technique of towing bergs is being developed in the North Atlantic where preliminary attempts are being made to tow icebergs out of the shipping lanes where they constitute a great hazard to shipping. Remember that the "Titanic" was sunk by an iceberg. Meanwhile, certain oil-rich Arabs are seriously investigating the possibility of bringing Antarctic icebergs to their dry lands. Several international conferences have been held dealing with the subject, technical studies have been done, and an actual attempt may be expected at any time.

The other variation on this idea is to use an iceberg as the base for a permanent residence in a more temperate region. The most appropriate region would seem to be in the 30's of south latitude of the Pacific Ocean. This is a vast area, entirely devoid of islands, with a pleasant climate, yet not too warm. New Zealand and New South Wales, Australia are located in this latitude. To make an iceberg into a permanent structure, the melting would have to be halted entirely. Exactly how to do this isn't known yet, but it doesn't appear to be an impossible goal. Erosion by sea water is the most critical hazard, so a covering would have to be applied below the water line. Effective insulation would have to be applied. And it might also be necessary to use artificial refrigeration, which could be powered by an ocean thermal power plant (OTEC), or perhaps by wind energy. Once the berg is stabilized, soil could be imported, and agriculture could begin.

The advantages of icebergs over artificial islands are that they would probably be cheaper per unit of area than any artificial structure. The berg itself would cost nothing, of course, but there would be transportation expenses, the cost of installing insulation, perhaps a refrigeration system, and of outfitting it in general to make it habitable. Also, a berg contains a huge supply of fresh water which could be used judiciously from the ice that is removed as tunnels are dug out to create living space. And there is a vast supply of suitable icebergs available with more being created every year, as they break off of the inexhaustable Antarctic ice shelves.

To begin, this concept should be developed and proved on a small berg, and then additional, larger bergs could be utilized. In time, it is conceivable that a huge and populous community could be created, one that freedom seekers would find more acceptable than any existing nation. This free "new country" would be inhabited by people living on ice islands, located in parts of the Pacific and other oceans, which are now entirely devoid of human habitation.

For more information, see:

ICEBERG UTILIZATION, edited by A.A. Husseiny, Pergamon Press, Fairview Park, Elmsford, New York 10523, 1978.

THE ANTARCTIC, by H.G.R. King, Arco Books, New York, 1969.

"World's Biggest Moving Job -- Icebergs!" by E.D. Fales, Jr., in January 1978 POPULAR MECHANICS. *Tells what is presently known about towing icebergs, mostly in connection with hauling Arctic bergs out of the shipping lanes of the North Atlantic.*

CHAPTER 4

LIVE ON A SUB-ANTARCTIC ISLAND

Far to the south, scattered across the Southern Ocean, up to the icy cliffs of Antarctica itself, lie a number of little-known, rugged, uninhabited islands. These sub-Antarctic islands are generally cold, barren places with not much plant or animal life, howling winds, and a lot of ice and snow. The coldest of them have a truly Antarctic climate, with virtually no animals or plant life, but the sea life is often abundant, including seals, penguins, sea birds, and fish and whales in the ocean nearby. The milder sub-Antarctics have some plant life, including tussock grasses and kerguelen cabbage, and some introduced land animals such as rabbits, rats, mice, ducks, and reindeer. The only people on any of these islands are researchers at occasional scientific stations. Families, including wives and children, are not to be found making their permanent homes in the Antarctic region. A main advantage of settling on one of these islands is that no one would expect to find you there. But that doesn't mean that life is impossible there. Explorers and scientists have led the way and have developed survival techniques suitable to this region. Perhaps now the time is ripe for settlers to come in and put down more permanent roots there.

There is one thing we should keep in mind, when considering the possibility of living on one of these generally unpleasant islands: Modern technology allows us to depend less on the natural environment than was the case in earlier ages. Now we can design a "built" environment that has any features we would like to include in it. For instance, on several of these islands caverns could be dug into the rock and any kind of environment we like could be built there. If you would like a tropical garden, a reasonable facsimile of that could be built there. We should remember that humans have now lived in space and on the moon, which shows what we are capable of. The sub-Antarctic islands, like almost any other earthly environment, is less hostile to human life than outer space is. At least on Earth we have air to breathe, and we don't have to worry about our blood boiling in vacuum if our suits should spring a leak.

The one necessary requirement for the operation of any artificial habitat over the long term is that you have an adequate energy source to drive it. On many of these sub-Antarctics there are energy resources of wind, water power, and sometimes geothermal energy, not to mention fossil fuels that may be present, sufficient to meet any needs.

But rather than say any more in such general terms, let's take a tour of the sub-Antarctic islands and see what particular conditions occur in each place.

1) Falkland Islands. The Falkland Islands lie in the South Atlantic about 300 miles east of South America at 51 to 53 degrees S, 57 to 62 degrees W. They consist of two large islands, East Falkland and West Falkland, and 200 smaller islands with a total area of 4,700 square miles. The islands have a population of over 2,000, about half of whom live in the town of Stanley. The Falkland Islands are the administrative center for the British Antarctic possessions.

2) South Georgia. South Georgia is a mountainous, barren island about 100 miles by 20 miles, with an area of 1,450 square miles located at 54 degrees S, 37 degrees W, about 800 miles SE of the Falklands. Its highest point, Mt. Paget, rises to 9,625 feet. The climate is cold and damp with a mean annual temperature of 35° F, and a strong northerly prevailing wind. Vegetation is sparce. There are no trees and no native land animals, but sea birds and seals are abundant along the coasts. There is one small village, Grytviken, on the island where most of the population of 500 live. The island is a British possession.

3) South Sandwich Islands. The nine South Sandwich Islands lie about 450 miles southeast of South Georgia at 56 to 59 degrees S, 26 to 28 degrees W, where they form the eastern curve of the Scotia Arc. These islands, which have a total area of 120 square miles, are extremely barren, being mostly ice-covered, although there are numerous patches of bare rock. Due to sheer cliffs and heavy surf, landing by boat is difficult. The British used helicopters to survey the islands. Sea birds, seals, and penguins are found on the coasts. A notable feature of these islands is their extensive volcanic activity. There has never been any population, not even any research stations, on these islands.

4) South Orkney Islands. The South Orkneys consist of the large islands of Coronation and Laurie, and the smaller islands of Powell and Signy, plus a group of smaller scattered islands

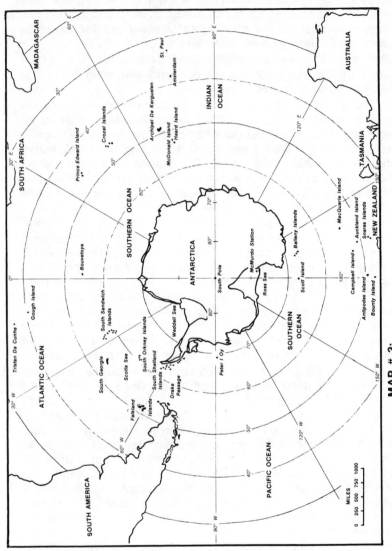

MAP # 3:

Antarctica, Showing Sub-Antarctic Islands

34

called Inaccesible Islands, all located at about 61 degrees S, 45 degrees W. The area of the whole group is 240 square miles. These islands all have a harsh, truly Antarctic climate, and only Signy is relatively ice-free. There is a British research station on Signy and an Argentine station (Orcadas) on Laurie.

5) *South Shetland Islands.* The South Shetlands are found at 61 to 64 degrees S, 54 to 63 degrees W, where they form the southern section of the Scotia Arc. These islands are mostly mountainous and ice-covered. The most notable member of the group is Deception, which is round, about nine miles in diameter, rises to 1,000 feet high, and is geothermally active. The center of the island consists of an open crater that forms a sheltered harbor, which was formerly a popular gathering place for sealers. Deception is relatively ice-free, and like all the south Shetlands, it has a mild climate for the Antarctic. Hot springs are found on Deception's beaches. Argentina, Chile, and Britain all had stations on Deception, but they were rapidly evacuated in 1967 when a volcanic eruption occurred. Now Argentina alone maintains a summer base on Deception.

King George Island, the largest of the South Shetlands, hosts three research stations: Beilinghausen (USSR), Arctowski (Poland), and Presidente Frei (Chile). There was also formerly a British station there at Admiralty Bay, which is now closed. Among the five other major South Shetland Islands, only one other, Greenwich, hosts a scientific station: Arturo Prat (Chile).

6) *Tristan Da Cunha.* Tristan lies in the middle of the South Atlantic at 37 degrees S, 15 degrees W, with the neighboring uninhabited islands of Inaccessible, lying 12 miles to the SW, and the three Nightingales Islands, 13 miles to the SSW. Of these only Tristan itself, which is part of the British colony of St. Helena, is inhabited. In 1961, volcanic eruptions forced the temporary evacuation of Tristan, but some Tristaners have since returned. The warm, wet climate of these islands is not at all Antarctic. Vegetation is lush, though the variety of species is limited. Sea birds abound.

7) *Gough Island.* Gough lies 230 miles southeast of Tristan (of which it is a dependency) at 40 degrees S, 10 degrees W. It has the same warm, wet climate and luxuriant vegetation. There are no land animals, but the island boasts a huge population of Rockhopper Penguins as well as seals and sea birds. There are

large guano deposits. Gough rises to 3,000 feet. It is uninhabited, but South Africa maintains a weather station there.

8) Bouvetoya. Located at 54 degrees S, 3 degrees E, Bouvetoya consists of a single cone of volcanic origin that rises to 3,068 feet and covers 19 square miles. Most of the island is covered by an ice cap, and the sky there is usually overcast. Snow falls frequently. Temperatures average about 29° F in winter, and seldom rise above 35° F in summer. Vegetation is limited to mosses and lichens. The island is inhabited mainly by seals and penguins, but no people, and is a possession of Norway.

9) Prince Edward Islands. Moving along to the Indian Ocean, we come to the Prince Edward Islands group, at about 47 degrees S, 38 degrees E, 900 miles southeast of Capetown. This group consists of two islands which are the double peaks of an underwater volcano. The larger island is Marion, about 84 square miles in area and rising to an altitude of 3,890 feet. The smaller of the two, at about half this size, is Prince Edward Island, lying just to the north of Marion. The highest elevation of Prince Edward Island is 2,370 feet. The climate is stormy and cloudy with frequent rain, and there is permanent snow on Marion above 2,000 feet. The vegetation consists of grasses and mosses and Kerguelen cabbage. Seals and penguins are plentiful. The group is a possession of South Africa, which has a weather station on Marion.

10) Crozet. The Crozet Islands are a French possession that lie about 1,500 miles southeast of Africa at 47 degrees S, 38 degrees E. They consist of two groups about 60 miles apart. Two islands, Possession and East, form the eastern group. The western group consists of one large island, Hog Island, and two small islets, the Apostles and Penguin. The islands are mountainous with East rising to 6,500 feet. The climate is marked by constant westerly winds (as they are in the "roaring forties" of latitude), but there are few glaciers. The vegetation is mostly tussock grasses, mosses and lichens. The coasts are crowded with seals, penguins and sea birds. The water around these islands are noted for dangerous reefs, which, along with the stormy weather, have caused many wrecks. There is a weather station on Possession.

11) Amsterdam. This French island, also known as New

Amsterdam, lies in the Indian Ocean 2,800 miles off the African coast and 1,200 miles northeast of Kerguelen at 38 degrees S, 78 degrees E. It is a mountainous island, 6 miles by 4 miles, with an area of about 16 square miles and its highest elevation at 2,760 feet. Wild cattle herds roam the island, and sea lions breed on the shore. Fishermen and whalers sometimes visit and a weather station was installed there in 1950, but otherwise , Amsterdam is uninhabited. Note its low latitude, which puts this island outside the sub-Antarctic region.

12) *St. Paul.* St. Paul, also part of the French Southern and Antarctic Lands, lies just south of Amsterdam at 39 degrees S, 78 degrees E. It is a smaller island, 3 miles by 1½ miles, with an area of 3 square miles, and consists of a broken volcanic crater which has been invaded by the sea. The island rises to 1,618 feet and has numerous hot springs. The surrounding waters abound with langoustes, seals and fish. The island was the site of an unsucessful settlement in the 18th century. A langouste canning factory operated there from 1908 to 1939.

13) *Archipel de Kerguelen.* This French archipelago lies in the south Indian Ocean at 48 to 50 degrees S, 68 to 70 degrees E. Kerguelen consists of over 300 islands, the largest of which is the triangular island Desolation, which is 100 miles long, with an area of 2,600 square miles. The coastline of this main island is deeply indented with many fjords, large bays dotted with islets, and many peninsulas. Inland, the island is cut up into numerous valleys and ridges. Mt. Ross, the highest peak, reaches 6,430 feet and has a permanent ice cap with glaciers flowing down from it. One third of the island is covered with ice. There are numerous small rivers and lakes fed by glacial meltwater and the abundant rainfall. The climate has only a small seasonal temperature variation with a summer average of around 40° F, and a winter average of 37° F. Rain or snow falls on up to 300 days a year and the sky is always at least partly overcast. Strong westerly winds prevail with gusts up to 100 mph. In short, it is a chilly, damp, drizzly place with lots of wind and not much sunshine.

Plant life is dominated by tussock grasses and the edible Kerguelen cabbage, and mosses and lichens. Offshore there are large patches of kelp. The land animals include reindeer, wild hogs, rabbits, dogs, rats and mice. Along the shore one finds penguins, seals, sea birds, and ducks. Available resources include peat bogs, lignite and guano. Kerguelen has been used as a sealing and whaling base. Attempts at raising sheep there were abandoned in the 1930's. Now the French maintain one tiny scientific station at Port-Aux-Francais, otherwise the entire archipelago is uninhabited.

14) Heard. About 300 miles southeast of Kerguelen at 53 degrees S, 74 degrees E, one finds Heard, a circular mountain rising from the ocean. It has an area of 225 square miles and its summit, known as Big Ben, rises to 9,005 feet. A permanent ice cap covers most of the island ending in sheer cliffs at the coast. There is some simple vegetation in a few ice-free spots, but not much. The usual sea life is found along the coasts. The island belongs to Australia which maintained a weather station there until 1955.

15) McDonald Islands. About 20 miles west of Heard lie the McDonald Islands which are an unexplored rocky outcrop, also under Australian sovereignty.

16) Snares Islands. Over in the Pacific Ocean lie the Snares, a group of uninhabited islets at 48 degrees S, 167 degrees E. They are distant outliers of Stewart Island (56 miles to the north) which is the most southerly of the New Zealand islands. The Snares consist of one large triangular island, with several offshore islets and a string of bare, rocky islets running off to the southwest above a rocky reef known as Western Reef. The main island, whose highest point is 620 feet, is bounded by steep cliffs on the west and south, and slopes down to the northeast where there is a good anchorage. The weather is windy, cloudy, wet and cool. The vegetation runs to stunted forest with patches of coarse tussock grass. There are widespread beds of peat impregnated with bird dung. Sea birds and seals are found there, but there are no introduced mammals. The island is now a seal sanctuary.

17) Antipodes. At 50 degrees S, 179 degrees E, which is almost the antipodes of London, lies this rocky, uninhabited group. The Antipodes have a total area of about 24 square miles and consist of one large island, Bollons, and several offshore islets and rocks. Bollons, 5 miles by 3 miles, is a plateau bounded by steep cliffs. Its highest point, Mt. Galloway, rises to 1,320 feet. The surface is rough, with a widespread blanket of waterlogged peat and swamps in the hollows. Tussock grass predominates.

18) *Bounty Islands.* About 490 miles east of New Zealand, at 48 degrees S, 179 degrees E, lie the Bounty Islands, a group of 15 small granite islets, with a total area of about one-half square mile. These are the barest, bleakest, and most desolate of New Zealand's islands. They have no natural vegetation, and no fresh water. Vast numbers of sea birds nest there.

19) *Auckland Islands.* The Auckland Islands, at 51 degrees S, 166 degrees E, are larger and more habitable than New Zealand's other sub-Antarctic islands. The plant and animal life there is comparatively lush for such a high latitude, and the islands have no permanent snow or ice. Lying about 200 miles southwest of New Zealand, the group consists of one large and 5 small islands with several islets and rocky pinnacles. The main island, Auckland, has an area of 179 square miles; Adams has 35½ square miles of area; Enderby has 1,770 acres, and Ewing and Disappointment are smaller. Auckland Island is 24 miles by 3 to 16 miles, and rises to just over 2,000 feet. Its west coast is a long, unbroken line of high cliffs, but the east coast is deeply indented with long, narrow inlets which provide many good harbors.

The climate is cool (35° to 65° F), humid, cloudy and very windy. There is shrubby forest at low altitudes, while above 300 feet there are open patches of tussock and sub-Antarctic meadow. The soil is peaty, waterlogged and sour. These islands boast fur seals, elephant seals, seabirds, penguins and parakeets.

In 1849, a settlement was attempted on Auckland, but the settlers were defeated by the hard conditions. Then in the 1890's sheep and cattle were grazed for a time, but the isolation of the islands led to abandonment of the enterprise. A few wild cattle, pigs and goats survive. Except for a brief occupation during WWII, these islands have remained uninhabited since.

20) *Campbell.* Campbell is a solitary island five miles wide and semi-circular in shape, with a bay on the northwest side, lying southeast of the Aucklands at 53 degrees S, 169 degrees E. It has an area of about 44 square miles. Campbell doesn't rise as high as the Aucklands, and vegetation is less abundant on its bare and scrubby hillsides. This is largely due to the activity of

wild sheep, left behind by an attempted farming settlement that was abandoned in 1929. The climate is characterized by a strong west wind, frequent rain and cloud, low temperatures, but not much snow or frost. The usual seals and penguins are abundant. Campbell is a New Zealand possession, and the government has maintained a weather station there since the 1940's.

21) McQuarie. Lying midway between Australia and Antarctica at 55 degrees S, 159 degrees E, McQuarie Island is a rocky mountain range rising from the sea. The main island is 21 miles by 3 miles, with an area of 46 square miles, and its highest elevation at 1,421 feet. Offshore lie two small uninhabited groups known as Bishop And Clerk, and Judge And Clerk. The waters surrounding abound in rock ledges which have caused many shipwrecks. Westerly winds blow constantly and reach speeds of over 100 mph. Rain or fog occur on over 300 days a year. But the island is free of ice and snow in summer. There are no trees, but plenty of scrubby vegetation, including the rhubarb-like McQuarie Island cabbage. Giant seaweed is abundant offshore. Seabirds, seals and penguins are now plentiful, since the Australian government has made the island a wildlife sanctuary, although many species were formerly hunted almost to extinction there. Since the 1940's, the Australian National Antarctic Research Expeditions have maintained several scientific research stations on McQuarie.

22) Peter I Oy. Peter I Oy lies 210 miles from Antarctica in the Bellingshausen Sea, at 69 degrees S, 91 degrees W. It is about 6 miles by 15½ miles and is entirely covered with ice and snow. The island's highest peak is Lars Christensentopp which rises to 4,003 feet. Peter I Oy is a Norwegian possession.

23) Scott Island. This tiny New Zealand island lies 310 miles from Antarctica at 67 degrees S, 180 degrees W. It is only ¼ mile by ⅛ mile in size, is surrounded by steep cliffs, and is entirely covered with ice.

24) Balleny Islands. The six islands of the Balleny group, which include Sturge, Young, Buckle, and Sabrina, lie about 160 miles off Antarctica at 69 degrees S, 159 degrees E. They are thickly covered with ice, and mountainous, with highest elevations ranging from 600 feet to over 4,000 feet. In the 1960's, a New Zealand expedition made helicopter landings in the Ballenys because they are so inaccessible from the sea.

To summarize some notable features of the uninhabited sub-Antarctic islands: The largest islands are Kerguelen, 2,600 square miles; Heard, 225; Auckland, 179; and Marion, 84. The warmest of these islands and also those with the most abundant vegetation are Inaccessible and the Nightingales (near Tristan), Gough, Amsterdam and St. Paul, and Auckland. The islands on which settlements have been attempted (which suggests that they may be the most habitable) are: St. Paul, Kerguelen, Auckland, and Campbell.

Here are some additional points concerning living on a sub-Antarctic island: On almost all these islands abundant food is available along the coast and in the sea. Various animals could be hunted or herded on some islands, such as sheep, cattle, or reindeer, and small mammals such as rabbits could be raised almost anywhere. Fruits and vegetables could be grown in greenhouses during the summer and perhaps even in winter on most of these islands. Due to the moderating effect of the ocean, on most of these islands even winter temperatures don't fall to Antarctic frigidness. Drinking water is abundant on most islands, as a liquid on some and frozen in ice and snow on most of the others.

The region is rich in energy resources. Tremendous wind-power is available the year round on most islands. Water power could be harnessed in some places, such as Kerguelen, which also has deposits of lignite (soft coal). And deposits of peat, which can be burned for fuel, have been found on Kerguelen, Snares, Antipodes, and Auckland. Geothermal energy, which can be used directly for heat and to generate electricity, has been reported on the South Sandwich Islands, at Deception in the South Shetlands, Tristan da Cunha, and St. Paul. Solar energy would be a useful resource on the warmer of these islands, but it is a marginal resource on those farther south which tend to be cloudy and overcast much of the time. Finally, a nuclear power plant could be set up anywhere, like the one that formerly provided electricity to McMurdo Station in Antarctica.

Security would be excellent in the easily defended, rugged terrain of these islands. In some places concealment could be made nearly perfect if settlers simply let snow and ice accumulate over their artifacts. And, of course, underground construction, which may be desireable anyway due to the climate, would be safe from spying eyes. This ease of concealment on many islands enhances the prospects of settlers who choose not to seek permission of the titular owner (government), or of those who go in anyway after permission to settle has been denied. For example, Kerguelen, with its 2,600 square miles of ridges and valleys, inlets and islands, is such a large, rugged and remote place that a party of settlers could quite easily evade detection, even if the French authorities order them to stay out.

Mobility and transport would pose difficult problems on many of these islands. Sea ice is an obstacle to ships in the more southerly islands and many of them have shorelines that make landing by boat quite hazardous. Air transport is complicated by high winds, freezing temperatures and mountainous terrain with no flat places for landing fields. Helicopters can land vertically, but are expensive to operate. Airships (blimps) can also hover and descend vertically and are cheaper to operate than helicopters, but windy conditions impede their operations also. Even so, airships may be the best transport solution in many cases. Overland surface travel on these rugged islands would also pose quite a challenge.

The cost of setting up a settlement would be in the high range on the most inhospitable of these islands, because a nearly complete artificial environment would have to be built. On some of the warmer islands settlers could live closer to nature using less exotic technology and that would cost less. People usually move into a previously unoccupied area for the purpose of exploiting the resources found there. And the Antarctic has vast mineral, energy, and sea resources that could be exploited and exported to provide income for settlers. The success of settlements that rely on an extractive economy depends on economics. To succeed, they would have to overcome the high costs inherent in this difficult environment and still deliver their exports to markets in the north at competitive prices.

On the other hand, a settlement which is intended primarily as a political refuge, where freedom seekers can find the liberty they passionately desire, need not depend as much on world economics. Such a settlement can be designed to achieve a large degree of economic self-sufficiency, so it would not depend on a large income from sale of its exports. In fact, a political refuge, especially one that was established illegally, may choose an isolationist policy for security reasons, and refuse to export to world markets at all. However, this would necessitate a more primitive lifestyle since it would prevent them from importing much technology from outside, because they wouldn't have the offsetting exports to pay for imports.

One more factor appears likely to have a significant impact on these islands, not to mention the rest of the world: As we burn increasing amounts of fossil fuels (coal, oil and gas), in effect we take carbon that has been buried in the earth and release it into the atmosphere as carbon dioxide. Atmospheric carbon dioxide has the ability to trap solar energy. (This is known as the greenhouse effect.) So the result of increasing the percentage of carbon dioxide in the atmosphere (which has risen 10% in the last 100 years) is to produce a warmer climate all over the globe. This has two major effects: One is that weather patterns will be changed all over the world. The second is that glaciers and icecaps will melt, raising the level of oceans and drowning coastal areas (including cities) and low islands. Some now-fertile areas will become deserts; some deserts will bloom. Sub-polar areas especially will become milder and more habitable.

As weather patterns shift faster than farmers can adapt, food production will be disrupted. Famines will follow. As governments struggle to feed their populations and to maintain their geo-political status, wars will break out.

When will all this take place? Scientists calculate that a doubling of the atmospheric carbon dioxide level would trigger these events, and they expect that to happen within the next 20 years. The only way to prevent it is to greatly cut our consumption of fossil fuels. That seems highly unlikely.

What effect will this have on the sub-Antarctic islands? For one thing, these remote places start looking all the more attractive as refuges, well away from the coming global turmoil. And since most of the world's population live north of the equator, that is where the worst of the trouble will be. Because weather patterns generally don't cross the equator, if there is a nuclear war in the north, southern regions will be less affected by fallout. Furthermore, as the weather gets warmer, climatic conditions will improve on the sub-Antarctic islands, glaciers will melt, growing seasons will lengthen. It is true that the rising sea level will be a negative factor. But the rise will be gradual, only tens of feet at first, although it might eventually reach up to 200 feet when all of the Antarctic icecap, which contains 90% of the ice on Earth, has melted. However, that will take some time to happen. So, while coastal areas will be submerged, and low islands will disappear under the waves entirely, the centers of high islands will not be affected. Perhaps now is the time to get in on the ground floor of the coming boom in higher elevation sub-Antarctic real estate.

On the other hand, the actual temperatures that have been measured indicate that the world has been in a slight cooling trend since the 1940's. And some observers have predicted that we are entering a new ice age. Maybe the rising carbon dioxide level will soon overcome the factors causing the cooling. Or maybe we will be very lucky and the two tendencies will just balance each other out. You can choose whichever future you think is more likely.

Regardless of what the future may hold, any people who settle on a sub-Antarctic island now must be prepared to work hard and to put up with rough conditions in the beginning. They must be willing to endure long periods of isolation, especially through the long nights of the southern winter. But there is good reason to think that quite a comfortable lifestyle could be developed in time. And if any one of the many possible catastrophes should do in the civilized world, a sub-Antarctic home might be the key to survival. Among the necessary requirements for a sub-Antarctic settler will be an optimistic attitude which sees the challenge and adventure and beauty in this austere and rugged environment.

For more information, see:

THE ANTARCTIC, by H.G.R. King. Arco Books, New York, 1969. *Besides its discussion of Antarctica, this book has a chapter describing in detail each of the sub-Antarctic islands.*

AN ENCYCLOPEDIA OF NEW ZEALAND, edited by A.H. McLintock. *This three volume reference work, published by the government of New Zealand, contains excellent descriptions of all the sub-Antarctic islands lying near New Zealand.*

WEBSTER'S NEW GEOGRAPHICAL DICTIONARY, published by the G and C Merriam Co, Springfield, Massachusetts, 1972. *A dictionary of geographical places around the world, including islands, with a brief description of each.*

PART II

LIVE ON THE OCEAN

CHAPTER 5

LIVE ON A FLOATING PLATFORM ON THE OCEAN

Recently an ad appeared in the *Wall Street Journal* offering office space on a modern, fully stabilized ocean liner, sailing under Panamanian registry, and anchored in international waters just 20 miles out from New York City. The ship would be leased from an established steamship line and would be operated by a fully licensed professional crew. Its offshore location would put the ship outside the US Government jurisdiction, but it would be close enough to shore that land phones and shuttle service to shore would be available. Thus the ship would provide the legal advantages of a tax haven combined with the convenience of proximity to the US metropolis. Rents would be in the $50 to $100 per square foot per year range, which is similar to the cost of modern office space in a Carribean tax haven and compares to about $20 per square foot in New York City.

It should be emphasized that there is nothing illegal about this proposal and no grounds for the US Government to oppose it. While activities might take place on board this ship which are not legal to do inside US territory, this should be no more a matter of US Government concern than if such activities were to occur in Bermuda, or the Bahamas, or in any other foreign country.

This offshore location might be especially suitable, for example, for physicians wishing to set up a clinic to practice therapies not presently allowed in the US, such as treatment with Laetrile or other treatments now in use in other countries which are not yet approved for use in the US because the years-long government approval process has not yet been completed. Another use for such a ship would be for an offshore commodity exchange which would stand outside the increasingly strict regulatory climate in the US.

There are numerous advantages to living on the open sea (outside government jurisdiction), whether on an ocean liner, or on some kind of floating platform. For one thing, taxes would be greatly reduced. There would be no state income tax, no sales tax, use tax, property tax, excise taxes, etc. But the situation regarding federal income tax is somewhat complicated. The US

Government levies income taxes on all income earned by anyone within the US. Also, US citizens must pay income tax to the US on any income earned outside the country. The US is the only nation that makes such a demand. However, if you stay outside US jurisdiction, the US Government can't legally force you to pay what they say you owe them. But if you ever expect to reenter US territory, you should have paid what they say you owe, or you risk being arrested. If you are, or become, a non-US citizen, and if you live and earn your income outside the US, then the US Government will make no further claim on you. And a non-US citizen earning only foreign income can visit the US as a tourist without being hassled about US income taxes.

Another benefit you would enjoy on the open sea is mobility. If your home is on a ship, you can sail to any part of the world you please. an unpowered floating platform can be towed anywhere. You can stay in any one place for as long as you like, and move on when you like. Your home can be anchored just outside any of the world's great seacoast cities, or alternately, you can linger just off an uninhabited coast or island.

Many of the problems of on-shore living can be left behind when you take to the sea. There are no muggings or burglaries on the open sea, no big city noise, no air pollution, no dangerous traffic, no streets being torn up for repairs. You won't have to look at decaying slums or dismal public housing barracks when you can enjoy an ocean view on all four sides. And yet, if you locate just outside a major population center, all the amenities of big city living would be easily accessible to you. A short trip by boat or helicopter would bring you ashore. There you could connect with any means of transportation to rapidly travel anywhere in the world. You could send your children to schools ashore and pay tuition for only the services you use. You won't have to pay school taxes to support facilities that you have no use for. And if you like, you can keep your children out of school and educate them at home, without violating any laws. It's entirely up to you. The local shops, sporting events, and all other entertainment is just as easily available to you.

Meanwhile, at home on the open sea, all water sports are available year round. You can swim, fish, or go boating just outside your own front door.

If you run a business on the open sea, you would enjoy additional advantages. There are tax benefits: no federal tax on corporate profits, no state corporation tax, no social security tax. And any open sea facility is a free port. You can bring in any raw materials and ship out any finished products, without paying tariff duties.

Outside government jurisdiction on the open sea, there are no regulatory agencies to contend with. You can dispense with the expense and bother of excessive paperwork, forms and reports. You won't be ordered to waste your time appearing before government bodies. Licenses and permits will be things of the past. Government litigation and harassment, and the uncertainty caused by changing laws, regulations, and interpretations will be eliminated.

A floating place of business has all the watery surface of the Earth to choose from for its location, including sites just a few miles from major markets and transportation centers. So you can find a site close to your market, to your labor supply, and to your source of raw materials.

An offshore location would make possible easy daily commuting by workers living nearby on shore. By selecting a suitable location, you can employ a large number of unskilled laborers who are eager to work, even for low wages. There would be no immigration barriers preventing workers from coming into your open sea workplace. Other skilled workers could live and work at your open sea location and remain outside any government's jurisdiction while there. In particular, non-US citizens could live and work at a site just off the US coast and not be subject to US income taxes or to any military draft as they would be if they were employed on shore. And yet they could travel freely within the US, to shop and play, as foreign tourists.

Labor relations on the open sea would not be subject to the labor laws of any government, so workers and employers could contract freely and set any terms of employment that they find mutually agreeable.

Developing the ability to live on the oceans opens for settlement the 70% of the Earth's surface that is covered by water. No government has jurisdiction over the high seas. Freedom of passage over the ocean is a tradition as firmly rooted in international law as any could be. With the growing interest in exploiting the resources of the seabeds, governments in recent years have been discussing the legal status of the oceans in several Law of the Sea conferences. But what is under discussion is the use and ownership of the sea bed. No one is suggesting any limitation on the right of free passage through and on the water above. Furthermore, these discussions seem to be in a long term deadlock between the developed nations, whose industries have the technology to exploit the seabed, and the backward countries that do not have this ability. The governments of these "third world" nations are demanding to be paid a share of the wealth recovered anyway, using the self-serving and socialistic argument that the resources of the ocean belong to everyone in common, and dismissing the traditional concept that unowned resources belong to the first person who can obtain and make use of them.

While this political squabble is going on, technology continues to advance. Oil drilling rigs are being used at increasingly greater depths. Some tower above the sea bed; others float on the surface and are held in place by anchors or by powerful engines. Several designs have been developed for artificial habitats in which people could live on the surface of the ocean. For example, William Barkley has designed a housing unit that he calls a "reefhome". This could be used as an individual family home, or as a school, factory, store, community center, etc. The reefhome would consist of a large diameter pipe section, suspended horizontally, in which living quarters would be built. A deck would be raised above the pipe section and would be connected to it by two hollow cylinders with circular staircases inside. Suspended on cables below the pipe section would be a concrete open-lattice mat. The unit would float at a depth such that the pipe section/living quarters would be below the surface (for protection from bad weather), while the deck would be above the surface, allowing free access to sunshine and open air. While the reefhome could be towed from place to place, it isn't really designed to be mobile, and it would usually be anchored in one place. The mat suspended below would add stability to the unit. Also, various forms of sea life would attach to and grow on the mat, and fish would gather to feed on them.

The reefhome could be made out of steel, fiberglass, or concrete. Steel would allow the fastest construction, but fiberglass would be lighter, and concrete would be the cheapest and the most durable. Barkley calculates that a 20 foot diameter by 100 foot long reefhome with rounded ends on the pipe section would provide 2,100 square feet of living space on the main deck of the living quarters, with more space on a lower deck in the bottom of the cylinder and perhaps a larger square footage than that again on the deck above the surface.

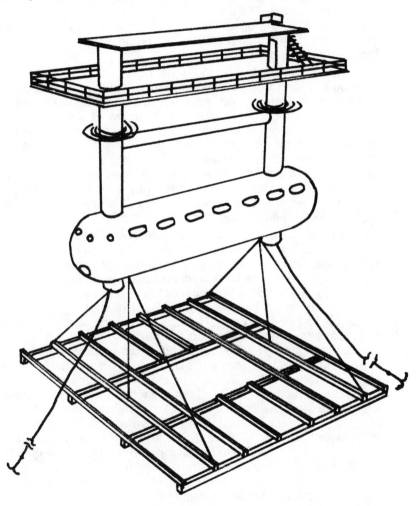

This above-water deck could be used for conventional gardening in containers, as a dock for boats, and perhaps as a landing pad for helicopters. We might think of it as the sea dweller's patio or back yard. The living cylinder below would be fitted with numerous windows, allowing easy observation of the underwater world. The artificial reef growing on the mat below would serve as the ocean settler's farm, providing a home for aquatic plant and animal life that would be a source of food for the humans residing below.

An artificial breakwall could be built around a group of floating platform homes like reefhome or some other design, to shelter them from rough seas. Or they could make use of naturally existing "breakwalls" in the form of coral atolls. A floating habitat could be anchored in the sheltered lagoon of any atoll, but the most interesting situation is to use the lagoon of an uninhabited atoll which may have only a small land area, or even to use a bare reef with no land area at all. Many bare reefs offer the added attraction that they are not even claimed by any government, and so they are available to the first pioneers equipped to use and defend them.

A typical bare reef is North Minerva Reef, which lies southwest of Tonga in the South Pacific. Minerva Reef is nearly round and about 3½ miles in diameter. The reef encircles a lagoon, but there is no land or any islands there. An approach is best made at low tide when most of the reef is visible. One sees waves breaking on the reef and dark rocks sticking out of the water up to five feet high. There is a straight, wide, fifty foot deep pass through the reef on the northwest side. Anchoring inside the lagoon provides protection from high seas, but there is no wind protection. Inside the lagoon there are patches with a sandy bottom at 25 to 50 foot depths. A reef such as Minerva forms an effective breakwall and yachts have successfully weathered storms with gale force winds while anchored in such places. (This description follows an eyewitness report from a letter dated June 5, 1978 from Sue and Don Moesly, on board their ketch *SVEA*, at Suva, Fiji Islands, which was published in Seven Seas Cruising Association Bulletin.)

The oceans are full of dozens, maybe hundreds of bare reefs similar to Minerva. However, Minerva itself is no longer a good prospect for ocean settlers to consider since it has now been claimed by the King of Tonga, following the abortive attempt to establish a new nation, which was to have been called the Republic of Minerva, there.

Another way that a bare reef or an uninhabited atoll could be settled is to use a large ship to create an artificial island. Consider what might be done with an oil tanker: At the present time there is an over-supply of oil tankers, many of which are being kept in storage in Norwegian fiords. It might be possible to purchase one of these surplus vessels at a price which is low for such a large ship. Even regardless of the supply situation, tankers, like all ships, have a limited useful life, and end up (if they don't sink first) being sold for scrap, when they get too old to profitably carry oil. After obtaining one of these ships, one would clean out the oil tanks and rebuild them into living quarters. Then the ship would sail to its chosen destination, which would be an uninhabited atoll or a bare reef similar to Minerva. Somewhere along the way, it would take on a load of topsoil. Before the converted oil tanker arrives at its chosen reef, an advance party would have opened a passage through the reef, probably with explosives, on the side away from the prevailing wind. This has been done in several places. The former tanker would sail into the lagoon, and find (or create) an anchorage with a level bottom at a suitable depth. The ship would then be carefully scuttled, so that it slowly sinks until it sits upright on the bottom at such a depth that its deck would remain at a desireable height above the high water mark. It would be firmly anchored in this position. Then the topsoil would be brought up from the hold and spread on the large flat deck of the tanker and suitable atoll vegetation would be planted, especially the highly important coconut palm. In this way, a large, artificial island could be created quickly, easily, and at relatively low cost.

Having completed its last voyage, the former tanker could convert its engines into a temporary community power plant. But it would probably be desireable to change over to the use of some renewable energy source rather quickly to eliminate dependence on imported fuel. Later, if the settlement grows and prospers, additional tankers could be added to the permanent fleet in the same way. Also, numerous other floating homes and vessels could join the community for a short or a long stay. Plenty of living space is available since even small atolls often have lagoons that are thirty square miles or more in area.

If we were to live at sea within a natural or man-made reef, in a floating platform such as reefhome, or on an artificial island, such as one made from a scuttled oil tanker, these are the conditions we would find:

The energy to run such a sea habitat would come from solar energy, wind energy, power from waves, or an OTEC (ocean thermal energy conversion system). An OTEC uses the temperature difference between warm surface water and cooler water from the depths to produce power. It is really a solar energy device that uses the surface of the ocean as a huge natural collector. There are three other ways to get energy from the ocean, which harness currents, tides, and differences in salinity, but these methods probably would not be as feasible at a mid-ocean site as along the coast of the mainland.

Food would be available in the form of fish, seafood, and seabirds, either captured from the wild or cultivated. The scuttled tanker would provide a large growing area on its soil-covered deck, on which salt-hardy plants could be intensively cultivated. The reefhome would allow some terrestrial plants to be grown in containers on its above water deck, but more food would come from the artificial reef suspended below. Ample fresh water could be made through solar distillation of sea water. Either the former tanker or the floating platform would provide a larger living space and greater stability than the cramped quarters one would have in a small boat, but the small boat would offer more security in the form of mobility: it could make a strategic withdrawal in the face of an overwhelming threat. By contrast, the scuttled tanker could not be moved at all. And while a floating platform such as reefhome could be towed to a new location, it couldn't slip away in the middle of the night as easily as a small boat could.

Security of one's person and property would be enhanced by the vast uninhabited area of the ocean that a settler would have to choose from, but the use of defensive force would still sometimes be required, so appropriate preparations would be a necessity. Small boats have been hijacked on the high seas. Their owners are never seen again, but the vessels sometimes turn up, being offered for sale, or being used by drug smugglers. The newspapers are full of stories of Thai pirates attacking Vietnamese Boat People in the South China Sea. And we hear of rapacious government actions like forces of the King of Tonga driving peaceful republic of Minerva settlers off the Minerva Reef. These are the kinds of aggressions that ocean settlers should be prepared to defend against. Living outside the sovereign territory of any government, ocean settlers would be on their own in matters of defense. But on the other hand, they wouldn't be paying taxes to support a bloated "National Defense" bureaucracy of questionable effectiveness, and this would leave them with more of their income free to spend meeting their real defensive needs.

The cost of constructing a floating habitat like reefhome would probably be modest, comparable to the cost of a small boat. The cost of obtaining an oil tanker and converting it into an artificial island would be much higher, but that cost would be divided among a community of people who would live there, rather than just a single family.

The income possibilities aboard a sea home include location-independent income such as from writing, and also exploiting marine resources. Later, as communities of ocean settlers come together, some people will be able to make a living providing the kinds of services that are in demand in any small community. In certain locations there may be underwater mineral resources that can be harvested and exported, and minerals could be extracted from seawater in any location, provided that sufficient energy was available, which could be supplied by an OTEC.

An ocean settler could choose to locate in any latitude and thus select any kind of oceanic climate he might want, from torrid to frigid. But I imagine most would prefer a subtropical location, perhaps in the thirties of latitude. Happily, there are truly vast empty ocean areas in such regions available for settlement.

The oceans remain one of the last relatively unpopulated and unpolluted regions on Earth. The technology which would enable humans to live on the oceans is now becoming available and use of this technology would make possible a high quality, comfortable and free lifestyle on this watery last frontier.

For more information, see:
"Home Is The Ocean", by Will Barkley, in REASON magazine, December 1972. *Gives more information about reefhome and other deep ocean structures designed by Barkley. You can inquire about the availability of this back issue by writing to REASON, Box 40105, Santa Barbara, CA 93103.*

CoEVOLUTION QUARTERLY No. 23, Fall 1979. *100 pages of this issue are devoted to people in relation to the oceans. Of greatest interest is "Ocean Arks" by John Todd (of New Alchemy Institute) in which he describes the vessel he is planning to build, a kind of greenhouse on a sailing ship, which would be a self-sufficient ecosystem. He intends to use this vessel to transport live fish and other organisms from places where they are abundant to distant markets. Such a vessel would in fact be another kind of independent floating sea home. This issue costs $3.50 from CoEVOLUTION QUARTERLY, Box 428, Sausalito, CA 94965.*

If you want to check the present status of the **offshore ocean liner project**, the promoters can be reached at this address: Open Sea, Erwin S. Strauss, c/o CRC, 4020 Williamsburg Ct, Fairfax, VA 22032.

"Offshore", 1200 S Post Oak Rd, Houston, TX 77056. *Journal of ocean business. Send $2.00 for a sample issue.*

"Ocean Industry", Box 2608, Houston, TX 77001. *Engineering, construction, operations -- send $2.50 for a sample issue.*

"Sea Frontiers", Magazine of the International Oceanographic Foundation, 3979 Rickenbacker Causeway, Virginia Key, Miami, FL 33149. *6 issues per year, annual membership $15.00.*

CHAPTER 6
LIVE ON A BOAT

One of the best ways to live free, and one that many people are already enjoying, is to knock around on a small boat. You could choose any of several variations on this basic idea. You could make long passages in a boat, travelling from port to port, or visiting uninhabited islands or remote coasts. Or you could stay around one coastal area like British Columbia, Canada, with its myriad islands and rugged inlets. Another idea is to hang around inland waters, living in anything that floats made up into a houseboat, in back bays, swamps, rivers, bayous, lakes, etc. A different approach is to use a derelict ship to create an artificial island. For example, an obsolete oil tanker could be taken to a bare reef in some tropical ocean and scuttled in the lagoon so that its deck is above water, to create an instant new island.

The main advantage of living on a boat sailing on the ocean is that you are free to do what you please, out from under bosses and bureaucrats and taxmen. If a boater gets hassled anywhere, he can hoist anchor and sail away. Waterways are great highways that open up the whole world to a boat equipped for ocean travel. Boat living provides the opportunity to earn income by engaging in such activities as fishing, salvage, carrying cargo (smuggling), and chartering. Above all, many people find that playing with boats is great fun.

Those who live on inland waters would be subject to the rules and regulations that the government of that place chooses to impose. But they've got to find you before they can tax or regulate you. And some of these watery places are so inaccessible that no government is going to waste all the effort and money it would take to dig out one harmless, free-spirited water rat. The world is three-fourths water with millions of square miles of oceans, bays, rivers, lakes, swamps, etc., and almost no one living there. It is impossible for the authorities to control more than a small part of it.

For more Information, see:

BOAT LIVING, by Jack Wiley, International Marine Publishing Company, 1976. *The author has drawn upon his four years of live-aboard experience to write this how-to book covering the details of living aboard all kinds of boats.*

LIVING ABOARD: THE CRUISING SAILBOAT AS A HOME, by Jan and Bill Moeller, International Marine Publishing Company, Camden, ME 04843. *This publishing company sells over 500 marine books and will send a free list upon request.*

CRUISING UNDER SAIL, by Eric Hiscock. Oxford University Press, 200 Madison Ave, New York, NY 10016. *Covers living aboard, maintenance, repairs, supplies, special sails, auto steering, coastwise navigation, anchoring, and more.*

VOYAGING UNDER SAIL, by Eric Hiscock. *Covers most of the same topics as his CRUISING UNDER SAIL, and also goes into ocean passages, with information on navigation, tools, etc. These books by Hiscock are considered the boating "doers" bible.*

"Pacific Islands Monthly". *A magazine filled with current news concerning Pacific islands, published in Australia. Of particular interest is PIM's regular column "Cruising Yachts" which relates news of activities of private yachts and their arrivals at and departures from various Pacific ports. To subscribe to PIM from mainland USA, send $18.00 to the US agent at 2812 Kahawai Street, Honolulu, HI 96822.*

The Seven Seas Cruising Association is an organization whose members (commodores) all live aboard their boats. They publish the *SSCA Bulletin* which consists largely of letters from yachters describing their voyages, experiences, and the places they visit. Non-members can subscribe to the bulletin by sending $10.00 to SSCA, PO Box 14396, North Palm Beach, FL 33408.

WATER SQUATTERS, THE HOUSEBOAT LIFESTYLE, by Beverly Dubin. Capra Press, 631 State Street, Santa Barbara, CA 93101. Published in 1975. *This is a photographic documentary about handmade houses afloat, dealing mainly with the west coast houseboat communities at Sausalito, Seattle, and the Sacramento delta.*

THE COMPLETE GUIDE TO HOUSEBOATING, by John W. Malo. MacMillan Publishing Co., New York, 1974. *Just as the title says, with an appendix listing books and magazines for further information.*

CHAPTER 7
LIVE ON A DESERTED ISLAND

Throughout the world's oceans there are hundreds, if not thousands, of uninhabited islands. Many are located in tropical and subtropical regions of the Pacific. By now all of these islands have been claimed by some government. But if one were to settle on certain of these islands, even with the knowledge and permission of the government, he would be free from much intrusion by the government simply because the island is so remote. Another possibility is for one to sneak into one of these places without anyone's knowledge or consent. Then you would be completely free from any government interference -- unless you were discovered.

Many empty Pacific islands are uninhabited for one of three good reasons: either they are barren sandy or rocky places where there is little vegetation, or they are active volcanoes, or they are tiny atolls with very little land area above sea level. Places like these are not very attractive prospects for settlement, but they do have the advantage that no one would expect to find anyone living there, so they probably won't come looking. This means that the hardy person who can devise a way to live in one of these places will have located quite a good hideout. And the sizes of these islands range from a couple dozen acres to several square miles, which is a larger acreage than most people could afford to buy or lease elsewhere. All of this space and all of the resources found there are available for a settler to use as he wishes, without anyone interfering, as long as he remains undiscovered.

Barren islands very often support huge populations of sea birds which could be used for food and fertilizer and anything else that a clever person could devise. On any dry island drinking water could be made from sea water using solar distillation. Or the occasional rainfall could be captured and held in cisterns. Otherwise, living on a barren island would require a nearly self-sufficient habitat similar to what one would need for living in a desert.

Rock islands offer tremendously good defensive possibilities. Among the strongest fortresses in the world are those cut into the rock at Gibraltar and on the Nationalist Chinese island of

Quemoy. Powerful guns mounted in caves dug deep into the rock are very hard to knock out. There are many empty rock islands in the Pacific that could be made into fortresses by any person so inclined, limited only by the amount of money he has to spend. One problem is that most rock islands have no good harbors. But many have flat areas on top and that suggests that an airship (blimp) would provide a good means of access to such a place.

Islands that are active volcanoes have very little going for them, except for the fact that geothermal energy is available there.

The small atolls offer another interesting option: A typical atoll consists of a coral reef that forms a ring around a shallow lagoon. The reef rises above sea level in some places and this forms the land area of the atoll. The interesting point is that even those atolls whose land area is only a few dozen acres or less in extent, have relatively large lagoons, often in the range of 30 to 50 square miles. So if one could provide the means to live on or under the water in the lagoon, and not just on the tiny land area on the reef, he would have all the living space he could use. Even the deepest lagoons are less than 200 feet deep, and "aquanauts" have already lived in underwater habitats at greater depths than that, which means that all lagoons are inhabitable using technology that already exists.

The greatest threat to life one would face on a small atoll is from tropical storms with high winds and from "tidal waves" (tsunamis). These winds and high seas have been known to strip an atoll bare of all vegetation. There is a report about how, during a hurricane in 1942, a man living on the small Pacific atoll of Suvarov had to tie his children to the largest tree on the island to keep them from being blown out to sea.

But the solution to this problem lies near at hand. Only a few feet below this maelstrom, beneath the water of the lagoon, relative calm prevails. This suggests that an appropriate strategy would be to build a storm shelter underwater in the lagoon. Then, when a tropical storm blows up, the islander could retire to the shelter and wait in safety for it to blow over.

Alternatively, the roles could be reversed and the underwater habitat could be made into one's main dwelling place. Then the underwater home would be the place where you actually live, and you could use the above sea level area of the atoll for recreation, growing food, etc. The land area could be left in a nearly natural state, which would make it almost impossible for outsiders to discover that someone was actually living there on the atoll.

But there are some deserted islands in the Pacific that are quite nice places to live even in conventional ways. For example, in the Marquesas Islands, which are part of French Polynesia, the two northernmost islands of Eiao and Hatutu are empty. They are large for uninhabited islands and physically very attractive. Eiao is 6 miles long by 3 miles wide and rises to an elevation of 1,889 feet. Located in the tropics at 8 degrees south latitude, it is covered with a tropical rain forest, but the higher elevations are somewhat cooler than the coast. At one time a Polynesian population lived there. Later the French used it as a prison island, but no one lives there now. Domestic animals were brought in during these previous occupations, and now sheep, cattle, pigs, and asses run wild on the island. Hatutu lies a few miles across a channel from Eiao and is somewhat smaller, about 4 miles by one mile, rising to 1,404 feet. Both of these islands lie 56 miles northwest of the populated island of Nuku Hiva, and they are well off the beaten track. It seems like it would be easy for a settler to survive on these islands eating the tropical fruit and other vegetation, hunting the animals for meat, and building with native materials. However, the French authorities probably would not allow westerners to settle on these islands. On the other hand, if one were determined to live there, perhaps the hardest part would be arranging transportation to the island. Once a resourceful person had taken up residence on Eiao, if he didn't want to be found, he could hide out in the jungle for years. It is the kind of rugged terrain where it would be all but impossible for the authorities to find a person who didn't want to be found.

Another excellent prospect is the Kermadec Islands on the other side of the Pacific near New Zealand. The Kemadecs are a dependency of New Zealand. The group consists of the island of Raoul (also known as Sunday) with an area of 11 square miles, and the smaller islands of Macauley, Curtis, L'Esperance Rock, and many smaller islets. The group has never had a native population. The only inhabitants now are about two dozen people who work at a weather station that New Zealand maintains on Raoul. There is no one on the other islands.

Physically, the islands have a quite pleasant, subtropical climate, with plentiful rainfall. The land is mountainous, fertile, and forested. There is a light easterly prevailing wind. The temperature ranges annually from about 82° F to 48° F. The main reason why there has been no settlement on these islands is because there are no sheltered harbors, and boats can only land in good weather. But it is interesting to note that Pitcairn Island, which has a very similar climate, also has no good anchorage, and yet Pitcairn has been populated for over 200 years.

My guess is that the New Zealand government might be persuaded to allow western immigrants to settle on one of the Kermadecs. Most likely they would hesitate only out of a concern that the settlers would get into trouble and have to be rescued by the government at considerable expense. Probably if the authorities could be convinced that you were well prepared and determined to make a go of it, they could be persuaded to give the project their approval. Or you could choose the other alternative and go in secretly without asking for permission. My opinion is that empty islands are unowned and belong to any persons who care to go there and make use of them. Sovereign governments take a different view of the matter, of course.

For more information, see:

UNINHABITED PACIFIC ISLANDS, by Dr. Jon Fisher, 1978. $5.00 postpaid from Loompanics Unlimited, PO Box 264, Mason,MI 48854. *A report by this author which describes over 80 deserted islands, telling about the history and physical conditions of each and including maps showing the exact location of each island. This is the first book to deal exclusively with uninhabited islands.*

AN ISLAND TO MYSELF, by Tom Neale. *Neale lived alone for about three years on Suvarov, an atoll in the Cook Islands and his book tells about his life there. Much detail is given about conditions on a typical atoll and what it is like to live alone on one.*

FATU HIVA, BACK TO NATURE, by Thor Heyerdahl, 1974. *Tells about the year (1936) that Thor, then 22, and his wife Liv spent living off the land on the southernmost Marquesas Island of Fatu Hiva. He gives extensive descriptions of climate, vegetation, and physical conditions on Fatu Hiva. While Fatu Hiva itself has a small popualtion, I mention this book because much of this* description also applies to the uninhabited islands of Eiao and Hatutu (about which no books have been written).

PITCAIRN ISLAND, by David Silverman, 1967. *A thorough description of the history and physical and social situation on Pitcairn. Pitcairn also has a tiny population, but I include this book because Pitcairn is quite similar to the uninhabited Kermadec Islands which are situated at about the same latitude. Also, anyone thinking about establishing a small community on an empty island would do well to study Pitcairn to get a taste of the social situation that is likely to result.*

WATER SQUATTERS, THE HOUSEBOAT LIFESTYLE, by Beverly Dubin, Capra Press, 1975. *This is a photographic report about the highly individualistic houseboat communities at Sausalito, Calfiornia and elsewhere. These communities are under attack by local government authorities who seem unable to tolerate anyone who chooses to live differently from the conventional herd. One solution for houseboat people would be to relocate to some deserted Pacific atoll. Looking at these pictures, you can imagine these bizarre and beautiful floating homes anchored in a distant lagoon, using the reef as a breakwall for protection against ocean waves, and using the land area and beaches as a backyard and playground.*

CHAPTER 8
LIVE IN AN UNDERWATER HABITAT

The planet Earth that we live on is primarily a water planet. 70% of the Earth's surface is covered with water, and all of this vast area is virtually uninhabited by humans. But many experiments have been conducted recently that demonstrate that humans can live in pressurized habitats at shallow depths underwater. This means that many underwater places, down to depths of several hundred feet of water, are now available to any adventurous pioneers who are daring enough to go and stake a claim. And many of these places are not controlled by any government, since governments are still squabbling about how to divvy up control of the oceans, and they may continue to argue about it for many years to come. And even those submerged places that are clearly within the jurisdiction of some government, such as continental shelves and inland waters, offer attractive sites to those who want to live free, because it should be easy to stay out of sight and beyond the control of the authorities while living in one of these places.

Here is a table summarizing some of the experiments in underwater living that have already taken place:

TABLE 1

Name	Year	Depth	Inhabitants	Duration	Sponsor
Conshelf I	1962	33 feet	2	7 days	J. Cousteau
Conshelf I	1962	200 feet	1	26 hours	E. Link
Conshelf II	1963	36 feet	5	30 days	J. Cousteau
Conshelf II, Deep Cabin	1963	90 feet	2	7 days	J. Cousteau
Conshelf III	1965	328 feet	5	21 days	J. Cousteau
SPID	1964	432 feet	2	49 hours	E. Link
Sealab I	1964	193 feet	4	11 days	US Navy
Sealab II	1965	205 feet	10	15 days	US Navy
Sealab III		450 feet			US Navy
Tektite I	1969	50 feet	4	60 days	US Government
Tektite II	1970	50 feet			US Government
Aegir	1970	200 feet	5	57 hours	Oceanic Foundation
Aegir	1970	516 feet	6	5 days	Oceanic Foundation

ABOUT TEKTITE II: Tektite II was sponsored by 9 government agencies, 25 universities and laboratories, and 6 industrial contractors. A total of 62 aquanauts were involved. 17 diving teams took turns in the habitat, various numbers of people for various durations. This was a 7 month experiment, in which the diving teams spent up to 30 days each on the sea floor.

ABOUT SEALAB III: Sealab III was never occupied. When it was placed on the ocean bottom in 1969, some leaks developed. Four divers went down to fix it, and one of them (as seen on a TV linkup) seemed to have some kind of seizure, which killed him. Later investigation showed that he had been asphyxiated by CO_2 due to defective equipment. The Sealab project was delayed while this death was being studied and apparently was never continued.

Let me describe one of these experiments in more detail. In 1963, Jacques Cousteau built Conshelf II, which was anchored on a coral ledge 36 feet below the surface in the Red Sea, 25 miles northeast of Port Sudan. It consisted of four structures: the main dwelling, known as Starfish House; a garage for the Diving Saucer submersible; a shed for tools and submarine scooters; and Deep Cabin, which was secured at 90 foot depth, with living space for 2 persons. Starfish House had four outer rooms and a large central salon. One of the rooms was a combination kitchen and laboratory in which meals were prepared. Men who were off duty relaxed in the salon. Along with the 5 aquanauts, a parrot named Claude lived in the habitat.

Claude provided a safety check on the air quality, because he would faint if the air went bad, long before humans would be affected by it. The men in the main habitat were under just twice surface air pressure, breathing compressed air, living in comfort. Two of the divers spent 7 days at Deep Cabin, and from there they made repeated dives to 165 feet. They breathed a mixture of oxygen, nitrogen and helium under almost four atmospheres of pressure. For Conshelf II, Cousteau assembled a team of average men, not especially young, not expert divers, who were chosen for their skills as cooks, mechanics, scientists, etc.

These experiments show that humans can live for long periods at depths down to several hundred feet, although as we will see, pesky problems still remain in deeper habitats. But the present state of the art will not permit living just anywhere under the ocean, since the tremendous pressure at abyssal depths is still greater than humans can endure with present technology, except for short visits in deep ocean submersibles.

Water and air pressure are the most important factors to consider when venturing underwater. At sea level the air pressure is 14.7 pounds per square inch, also called one atmosphere. Due to the great weight of water, water pressure increases rapidly as you go down to greater depths, at the rate of one atmosphere for every 33 feet of water. In the watery region from the surface down to 33 feet, called the first atmosphere of water, humans can swim safely with no equipment, rising to the surface to breathe. From 33 feet down to about 200 feet, which is six atmospheres of water, pressure suits and compressed air tanks are a necessity.

Below 200 feet, air, which contains 78% nitrogen, causes severe physical problems, so safer breathing mixtures have been developed for divers who work at these extreme depths. These breathing mixtures reduce or eliminate the nitrogen fraction and substitute helium instead, and they reduce the percentage of exygen from the 21% found at sea level down to about 5%. The high pressure offsets the lower percentage of oxygen so that the diver gets just the amount of this vital element that his body needs. With new breathing mixtures and other improvements, it is forecast that the range of free divers can be extended to a depth of about 1,000 feet. Below that the physical structure of the human body would be crushed by the pressure.

When scuba divers go below the first atmosphere of water, they breathe a gas mixture that is kept at a pressure equal to the water pressure at that depth. This is necessary because if the pressure inside his body were less than the water pressure outside, the diver would be crushed. Similarly, when habitats are lowered to a few hundred feet or less, they are pressurized to the same level as the water outside them. This makes it easy for the aquanauts to pass in and out of the habitat, but it also allows the habitat to be more lightly built, since it doesn't have to resist any substantial pressure difference. Explores who dive deeper to abyssal depths and into the deepest trenches of the ocean ride in vessels that are only moderately pressurized inside. These vessels have to be built with tremendous strength to resist the great difference in pressure.

Putting these deepest regions aside, let us look at the several kinds of shallow underwater places where human habitation is now possible:

a) *Continental Shelves.* Continental shelves are the areas along the seacoasts of continents, often hundreds of miles wide, which slope gradually down to about 600 foot depths, before falling off more sharply to the abyssal plains of mid ocean. Governments usually claim the continental shelves lying off their shores, but their area is large, probably millions of square miles in all. So it seems quite feasible for someone who didn't want to submit to the authority of the nearby government to keep that government from knowing about a habitat he might establish under the sea along the coast. Taking some pains to camouflage and conceal such a habitat would make it virtually impossible to find.

b) *Isolated Seamounts.* Away from the continents, there lie isolated mountains rising up from the ocean floor. If these mountains rise above sea level, they form islands. But many of these mountains do not rise above sea level, and these are called seamounts. Some seamounts rise close to the surface, and their peaks are at depths at which human habitation is now possible. No government presently lays claim to any deep ocean seamount.

Maps showing islands in the ocean give a misleading impression concerning government sovereignty. The lines you may see around some group of islands don't normally indicate the territorial boundaries of the government of those islands. lines are simply a convenient device the mapmaker uses to group together islands ruled by one government. Under present international law, only land areas above sea level can be owned by governments (or anyone), except for coastal areas. Governments claim to own their coastal areas underwater out to, formerly 3 miles, and now usually 12 miles. Lately many governments have proclaimed exclusive rights over 200 mile natural resource areas off their coasts, but apparently they do not claim full sovereign rights in these areas; they only claim the right to regulate and tax minerals, fish, and other resources that may be found there. Beyond 200 miles offshore, no ownership is now recognized.

So if one were to put a habitat on an underwater feature more than 200 miles from any land area above sea level, it would be

67

outside the claim of any government, under existing inter-national law. That doesn't guarantee that no government will try to run you off. Governments have been known to ignore legal fine points when they find it convenient to do so. But if, in addition, no one knew you were there, you would be safe from harassment. And being underwater, you would not be very visible. On the other hand, if some government did find you and initiated hostilities, a willingness to defend your property might be successful, especially if your opponent were some little two-bit island tyrant, with limited military resources.

A typical example of this kind of underwater feature is the Cobb Seamount, an extinct volcano that is located 270 miles west of the State of Washington in the north Pacific. Existence of the Cobb was not suspected until a US Fish and Wildlife Service officer found it in 1950. It lies well beyond the continental shelf, which puts it definitely outside US juris-diction. The upper slopes of the Cobb rise to about 120 feet below the surface and that gives it enough sunlight to support a lush growth of ocean plants and fish.

Several scientific organizations from Hawaii and Washington State have developed a plan, called Project Sea Use, to place an underwater habitat on the Cobb and thoroughly explore the summit. In connection with this project a US Coast and Geodetic Survey ship made a comprehensive survey of the Cobb in 1968, while divers went down for a closer look. At latest report, further work on the Cobb was awaiting funding.

c) Submerged Reefs. The submerged reef is another shallow underwater formation that can be found in many places throughout the oceans. These reefs are similar to the more widely known coral atolls, which consist of rings of coral surrounding shallow lagoons. When parts of the coral ring are high enough to rise above sea level, and to support vegetation and often a human settlement, that comprises a coral atoll. Submerged reefs have the same structure except that they have no habitable land area above sea level, though often some of the reef will rise above the water at low tide. Up to now these reefs have been of almost no use to anyone, and have been a hazard to shipping. But with the ability to live underwater in the lagoon of a submerged reef, a family or a tribe of aqua-pioneers could make such a place their home. An added attraction is the fact that most of these reefs have never been claimed by any government.

The following table lists a few typical shallow places in the Pacific Ocean where an underwater habitat could be placed. *(This is not a complete list.)*

TABLE 2

Name	Depth	Location	Latitude & Longitude
Cobb Seamount	122 feet	W of Wash. State in N Pacific	47N, 131W
Orne Seamount	96 feet	S of Tubual Islands	27S, 158W
Wachusett Reef	30 feet	S of Tubual Islands	32S, 151W
Wilder Shoal	18 feet	N of Howland	8N, 173W
Neilson Reef	12 feet	In Tubual Island chain	27S, 146W
President Thiers Seamount	60 feet	In Tubual Island chain	25S, 146W
Conway Reef	36 feet	S of Fiji	22S, 175E
Minerva Reefs	—	S of Fiji	21S, 159E
Kingman Reef	24 feet	In N Line Islands	6N, 162W
Keats Reef	48 feet	SE of Marshall Islands	6N, 173E

d) Uninhabited Atolls. Another promising site for an underwater habitat is in the lagoon of an uninhabited coral atoll. Since these lagoons are seldom more than 200 feet deep, they are entirely accessible to human habitation. The surrounding reef would shelter the habitat from ocean storms that sometimes do great damage to small atolls. And the land area of the atoll could be used for growing food, recreation, etc. Yet the habitat would be hidden beneath the water, out of sight of any unwanted visitors. The above-sea-level land area could be kept in an unimproved state so that it would not be apparent that anyone lived in the atoll.

For a typical example, consider Taka, which is an uninhabited atoll in the Marshall Islands. Taka has a reef 30 miles in circumference, but only 5 small islets with a total land area of 141 acres. The land area is so small that Taka will probably never be settled by people intent on living the usual atoll lifestyle. But notice that Taka's average-sized lagoon has an area of about 71 square miles, which is over 45,000 acres! Here is room enough for any size settlement, provided the settlers are willing and able to live underwater.

All uninhabited atolls with some land area, however small they may be, are claimed by some government. But settlers who don't want to submit to the jurisdiction of any government could probably remain undetected below the waves. One problem is that a small boat would be needed for travelling to and from the atoll. This would have to be hidden, if you are to remain invisible. Perhaps the boat could be drawn up on shore and hidden in the vegetation. Or a submersible vessel could be used which could be secured underwater. Another option is that the settlers could hire a yacht to drop them off before it continued on its way, provided they did not mind being stranded for long periods of time.

e) Inland Waters. Lastly, let's not overlook the possibilities closer to home in inland rivers and lakes, bayous, swamps, etc. A habitab underwater in such a place could be near an urban area and still well hidden. It would be much easier to get to than a home way out at sea. Perhaps one could even commute to an ordinary job from such a home. A secluded, well hidden "beaver lodge" beneath your favorite backwater could be built quickly and inexpensively. You might build it like a sealed watertight houseboat, with ballast tanks on the bottom. Tow it to your selected spot and open the valves to sink it.

The underwater dweller faces several unusual problems. The three most serious concern the air he breathes. These are related to "the bends", the percentage of oxygen, and nitrogen narcosis.

1) When a diver breathes compressed air, the nitrogen from the air dissolves in his blood and eventually penetrates to the marrow of his bones. When he resumes breathing air at normal pressure, he has to depressurize slowly, to give the excess nitrogen time to work its way out of his blood through his breathing. If he comes back to ordinary pressure too quickly, the nitrogen will form bubbles in the bones and joints. This is the painful and crippling disease known as "the bends", which may even be fatal.

The bends will be prevented if enough time is spent decompressing. The higher the pressure the diver has been under, the longer the time that is needed for depressurizing safely. Up to a week may be needed to decompress after the deepest dives. The US Navy has studied decompression extensively and publishes tables showing the necessary decompression rates for various dives.

Formerly it was thought that divers had to spend more time

decompressing depending on the length of time they had spent underwater. But then the phenomenon of saturation was discovered. If a diver stays at a particular depth (pressure) for long enough, his body becomes saturated with the gases he is breathing until he can absorb no more. Then it makes no difference whether he stays on the bottom for a day or a month - - the same length of time will be needed in either case for a safe decompression. Also, a saturated diver working at a certain depth can live in an underwater habitat and travel freely in and out of it without decompressing provided that the air in the habitat is kept at the same pressure as the water at that depth.

This decompression problem imposes a particular restriction on underwater communities. Travel between places at the same depth may be quite easy, but going to a place at a lower pressure (nearer the surface) will take a long time because you have to allow for decompression time. You could travel more quickly to higher pressure (deeper) places, but then it may take a long time (up to a week of decompression) to get home again. This would restrict travel and impede employment and commerce and the development of social relationships between people living at different depths. And another result is that communications facilities connecting different depths would be more widely used as a substitute for personal visits.

2) The second problem has to do with the percentage of oxygen. Air at sea level contains about 21% oxygen. When a diver breathes a gas mixture under great pressure, the percentage of oxygen must be reduced, say down to 5% for a certain depth, etc., so that the diver gets enough oxygen, but not too much. Too much oxygen can cause muscular twitching and convulsions; too little will lead to suffocation.

3) Nitrogen narcosis is another malady caused by breathing nitrogen under pressure; it is also known as "rapture of the deep". The symptoms are that divers behave as if drunk; they lose track of time, act irresponsibly, sometimes they even throw away their scuba gear and drown. This affliction is unpredictable and seems to affect some people more than others.

To eliminate some of the problems associated with breathing nitrogen under pressure, divers now breathe a helium and oxygen mixture when making deep dives. Helium, however, brings with it problems of its own. It is a rare gas, expensive, and not available in all parts of the world. Helium increases a diver's feeling of cold, so that he may feel cold at 85° F, when breathing helium. It also affects the vocal cords, making a person's speech sound like a squawking Donald Duck -- and this interferes with communication.

Other pesky problems involved with living underwater are that the air usually is very humid, which is uncomfortable and can cause rashes and softening of the skin. At 200 feet or greater depths a foam mattress and rubber sandles will flatten out, thin as a pancake. Aerosol cans will explode, while glass containers will implode. Peanuts will crumble to dust in a vacuum packed can. Lids have to be removed from jars, and from toothpaste tubes. Holes must be punched in canned goods, unless the contents include plenty of water. But the problems are less severe at shallower depths, say down to 30 or 40 feet, where divers breathe compressed air, without helium, as at Conshelf II.

There are some offsetting advantages of underwater living. It has been found that in a pressurized undersea habitat small cuts heal fully in 24 hours instead of a week. Beards hardly grow at all. There are no insect pests to bother with, and bad weather passes unnoticed above while conditions remain calm and serene in the depths.

My assessment of the present state of the art is that we now know enough about living at shallow depths, down to about 40 feet, that adventurous pioneers may now proceed to build homes down to that depth. Of course, a thorough study of the subject and plenty of scuba diving experience are necessary prerequisites. Below 40 feet, and especially at depths where special breathing mixtures containing helium are needed, residence is still too experimental, risky, and expensive to be attempted by anyone lacking extensive scientific and technological backup. At shallow depths, air and pressure can be supplied to a habitat with a simple air compressor. The difficulties of building a watertight structure should not be more than a determined amateur can overcome. And there are plenty of places where living at a shallow depth would provide a high level of security from potential coercers.

For more information, see:

UNDERSEA VEHICLES AND HABITATS, by Frank Ross, Jr. Crowell, NY, 1970. *Covers the history of diving, the techniques and equipment used in peaceful pursuits in the ocean excluding* warfare, but including many underwater habitats, and finishes with a chapter speculating on future developments.

COLONIZING THE SEA, by Erik Bergause. 1976. *A brief introduction.*

SECRETS OF THE SEA, by Carl Proujan, which is Part III of "The Last Frontiers". Doubleday, Garden City, NY, 1971.

SKIN AND SCUBA DIVING, A BASIC GUIDE, by Homer Gramling. The Ronald Press Co., New York, 1964. *Introduction to the fundamentals of skin diving, suitable for the complete novice, which could be used as the text of a basic course. Covers physics and physiology of diving, equipment, hazards, decompression procedures, and more.*

PRACTICAL DIVING, A COMPLETE MANUAL FOR COMPRESSED AIR DIVERS, by Tom Mount and Akira J. Ikehara. University of Miami Press, Coral Gables, Florida, 1975. *Provides advanced training and the latest state-of-the-art information on diving technology.*

THE GODWHALE, by T.J. Bass. Ballantine, New York, 1975. *This is a science fiction novel that dramatically portrays people living in underwater habitats.*

"Sea Technology" (magazine). Compass Publications Inc., Suite 1000, 1117 N. 19th St., Arlington, VA 22209. *Discusses design engineering, equipment, and techniques for providing services within the marine environment.*

CHAPTER 9
LIVE ON A SUBMARINE

Over 100 years ago, the science fiction novelist Jules Verne portrayed one of the ways humans could inhabit the oceans in his TWENTY THOUSAND LEAGUES UNDER THE SEA. In that book the mysterious Captain Nemo and his crew sail the world's oceans in the submarine *Nautilus*, going wherever they please, doing what they will, free from any outside authority.

In words that will strike a sympathetic chord in any true freedom-seeker, Verne has Captain Nemo say: "I am not what you call a civilized man! I have done with society entirely, for reasons which I alone have the right of appreciating. I do not therefore obey its laws." And Nemo's captive, Professor Arronax, muses: "Not only had 'Captain Nemo' put himself beyond the pale of human laws, but he had made himself independent of them, free in the strictest acceptation of the word, quite beyond their reach! ... No man could demand from him an account of his actions; God, if he believed in one - his conscience, if he had one - were the sole judges to whom he was answerable."

The instrument by which Nemo had liberated himself from the shackles of society was his submarine *Nautilus*. At the time when Jules Verne wrote his book, the first practical submarine was still some decades in the future. So when TWENTY THOUSAND LEAGUES... was written, Nemo's lifestyle was only a fantasy. Now it could be done.

The occupants of a live-aboard submarine vessel would be able to use not only the breadth, but also the depth of the oceans as their home territory. Even the fiercest storms would be of no concern because the submarine could slip below the towering waves to cruise in the peaceful depths. The sub could roam wherever its inhabitants desire, visiting friendly ports, or stopping at uninhabited coasts and islands. It could travel in polar regions and under icecaps. It could visit various shallow underwater places on a regular schedule if desired. The submariners could "stroll" through these watery parks wearing scuba gear and perhaps tend the vegetation growing there and harvest it for their food. In addition, various fish and other marine life could be hunted underwater. Or, imitating Nemo's

Nautilus, such a live-aboard submarine could tow a net behind and gather whatever the sea may offer to add to the food supply. To round out the larder, small terrestrial animals such as rabbits or chickens might be raised aboard in cages. And other delicacies could be gathered on occasional visits to uninhabited islands and coasts. Drinking water tanks could be filled from fresh water sources ashore when possible, or fresh water could be made by desalination of seawater if necessary.

It must be admitted that the cost of setting up a submarine habitat would be in the very high range. Some small subs are available commercially, but they are too small for living aboard. And they are quite expensive. For instance, Perry Ocean-ographic, Inc., of Riviera Beach, Florida, makes two to four person subs for prices ranging from $200,000 to $1.5 million. Up in Warren, Maine, George Kittredge is turning out a lower priced model at prices from $12,000 up. But his product is a one person minisub suitable for use as a "jeep of the deep" -- but not for living in. You can imagine what it would cost to custom build a submarine that would be big enough to live in for extended periods.

There is one way that it might be possible to acquire a large sub at a somewhat lower price. When aging Navy vessels reach the end of their useful life, they are stripped and sold for scrap to the salvage firms that break them up. The oldest US nuclear subs are now starting to be scrapped and it might be possible to acquire one at the scrap price. Of course, it would be sold gutted, without the nuclear powerplant or military hardware. It would need extensive rebuilding to make it seaworthy again, but you might still get a lot more for the money than you would get building entirely from scratch. One thing to remember is that military requirements are more stringent than civilian needs and a vessel may be scrapped more because the design is obsolete rather than because of actual deterioration.

When Jules Verne described his *Nautilus,* he spoke vaguely about it being powered by electricity which gave it fantastic powers compared to the existing surface vessels of that day. The nuclear powerplant of a modern submarine actually is capable of performing the wonders that were only fiction in Verne's day. Without a doubt, a nuclear reactor is the best energy source for a sub, leaving aside problems at both ends of the fuel cycle: preparing the fissionable fuel and disposing of radioactive wastes. But a nuclear power plant appears to be quite beyond the reach of a private owner at present. However, the second best submarine propulsion system, the diesel-electric engine, is a highly evolved design, which would probably be quite good enough for a civilian live-aboard vessel. However, having such a power plant does make the sub dependent on an outside fuel source. And that implies that the submariners will need an outside income with which to buy fuel as well as other necessities.

Captain Nemo had a large income from an underwater source, even though the *Nautilus* was so self-sufficient that no income was really needed. It seems that Nemo had located a sunken fleet of treasure ships off the Spanish coast, and he would stop there and withdraw a small fortune in gold and silver from this underwater "bank" whenever he felt the urge. Well, real treasure hunters know that finding sunken treasure isn't that easy, even if you have the technology to go down and walk along the seabed. But there are other treasures to be found in the oceans: minerals on the seabed, and living organisms to be harvested. Income may be earned in such activities. Up to now, our exploitation of sea life has been mostly at the primitive hunter/gatherer stage. It is about time we moved on in a big way into increasing the yield of the oceans through cultivation. A submarine habitat may be uniquely well suited to tending various submerged "farms" and "forests" whose output could be exported to balance the imports needed by the submarine economy.

Life aboard a free-roaming submarine would rank very high in security from any outside aggressor due to its concealment beneath the waves and its ability to rapidly leave any dangerous area. While the superpowers are rapidly increasing their ability to find submarines, the focus of their attention is on potential enemies with nuclear armaments. They are not going to waste their military resources keeping under observation non-threatening, lightly armed civilian vessels. And small nations don't have the ability to track submarines at all. With some small armament, and reasonably cautious procedures, a live-aboard sub should be able to easily defend itself against both private pirates and attempted government coercion.

We all have the impression that life aboard a submarine

requires squeezing through tiny spaces and living in cramped quarters. But we should remember that these space limitations are found on military vessels where the priority is to squeeze maximum firepower into the smallest space. A large crew is needed to operate all the equipment that is built into a military vessel. Furthermore, a warship must carry sufficient personnel to keep its stations fully manned around the clock with two or three complete shift changes. A civilian live-aboard sub would not have these same requirements. A private submarine would omit most of the weapons and a large part of the electronics. The crew size could be reduced both because operators are not needed for the gear that has been eliminated, and because round-the-clock watches by a full complement are not needed. Also, a high priority would be placed on providing generous-sized living spaces on a live-aboard private vessel, so the number of sub dwellers would be kept down to what the boat could easily accomodate.

What it comes down to is that life aboard a free-roaming private submarine would offer an ultra-modern, high technology, very comfortable lifestyle, which at the same time would be one of the freest, and most secure ways of life that can be achieved today.

For more information, see:

SUBMARINE, THE ULTIMATE NAVAL WEAPON, ITS PAST, PRESENT, AND FUTURE, by Drew Middleton. Playboy Press, Chicago, 1976. *As the title suggests, this is a thorough discussion of the history, present status, and future possibilities of the submarine as a weapon. For our purposes, this book reveals what is technically feasible to do with a submarine. It also shows the kind of vessels that may become available on the scrap market in future years. But, like most books about submarines, the focus is on military uses and the reader who is interested in peaceful applications must dig out the facts relevant to that use for himself.*

UNDERSEA VEHICLES AND HABITATS, by Frank Ross, Jr. Crowell, New York, 1970. *Describes various small subs that have been built for civilian use, especially in the oil and gas industry. Generally these are not big enough to live aboard. Also describes the immobile habitats in which people are living for extended periods underwater.*

TWENTY THOUSAND LEAGUES UNDER THE SEA, by Jules Verne. *The famous novel in which Verne speculates on what life would be like aboard a submarine whose inhabitants had completely severed themselves from people living on land. Inspiring, but it must be read critically because Verne wrote at a time when not much was known about undersea conditions, and many of his detailed guesses turned out to be wrong. The reader will also note that interpersonal relations within a small, isolated community, which is what a submarine would be, could not be as cold, isolated, and sexless as Verne describes life aboard the* Nautilus.

ILLUMINATUS! by Robert Shea and Robert Anton Wilson. Dell Publishing Co., New York, 1975. *This is a trilogy consisting of the three books THE EYE IN THE PYRAMID, THE GOLDEN APPLE, and LEVIATHAN, which portrays, in part, life aboard the fictitious* Lief Erickson, *a free and autonomous golden submarine. The* Lief Erickson *is far too grandiose and luxurious to be possible, and the way her passengers live is much more uninhibited, sexually liberated and downright bizarre than is likely to ever actually occur. But if you combine this book in your mind with Verne's TWENTY THOUSAND LEAGUES..., the kind of free submarine life that is really possible lies somewhere in between.*

PART III
LIVE AS A NOMAD

CHAPTER 10

LIVE AS A WALKING NOMAD

Although it may seem like a strange idea, the nomadic way of life is possible even in the North America of today. The key to making it work in the modern context is not to reveal that nomadism is your permanent way of life. Why look like a hobo and risk being hassled by every hick cop you might meet? Instead, why not be an upper middle class professional on a backpacking trip! But don't try to pass yourself off as an MD or someone with other useful skills that you might be called on to use in an emergency. Instead be an academic with a string of degrees in some obscure discipline, like "cultural sociobiology", or something. Then you can spout high sounding nonsense and impress the hell out of your listeners, without much risk of getting tripped up.

As a nomad you could be as free as you please, travelling the back roads, trails, inland waters, national parks, forests and mountain areas of North America (or elsewhere in the world, if you wish), going where you like, when you like, or stopping whenever you want for as long as you please. While the use of various vehicles offers certain advantages, the most flexible and the cheapest way to live as a free roaming nomad is to go on foot, carrying all your essentials in a pack on your back.

If you travel by walking, you could use the thousands of miles of hiking trails that have been developed throughout the USA. In the West, there are the Pacific Crest Trails that run along the mountainous spine of North America. In the East, the Appalachian Trail runs over 2,000 miles from Maine to Georgia. And then there are logging roads, little used back country jeep tracks, roads to ghost towns, etc. But there is no need to stay on the roads and trails when travelling on foot. "Shank's mare" is the most all-terrain "vehicle" there is. Just about every place on land is accessible to the walker.

The advantages of this way of life are many. You could get far back into the wilderness, away from most potentially coercive people. You could maintain almost no contact with government. You would have no real estate that government could tax or use to find you or to tie you down. You might have little income to interest government, but you wouldn't need much. And whatever income you do earn might well be in cash, which leaves no records. If you travel without a motor vehicle, you would have no contact with any department of motor vehicles, nor pay any registration fees or car insurance. You would live in intimate contact with the beauties of nature. You could travel mostly in unpolluted country, breathing clean air and drinking pure water. You would get plenty of exercise which would keep you healthy and promote a long life. You would set your own timetable, not be bound to someone else's schedule. You would be far away from the raucous demands of the rat race. Your life would be your own.

It really would take very little money to live this way. Think of having no rent to pay, no utility bills, no car payments, or car insurance. Your housing would be a good backpacking tent and whatever other temporary shelter you may find or build along the way. Much of the time you would be living out-of-doors with the whole world as your home and the sky for your roof. Clothing would have to be selected with greater concern for function and durability than if you were living a more common lifestyle, but it need not be any more expensive. Avoid fads and the dictates of style, and shop the used clothing stores for bargains. The purchased part of your diet would run from freeze-dried foods at the top end of the expense scale, down to grains and flours at the cheap end. Purchased foods would be generously supplemented with foods foraged along the trail, small animals taken with snares, and fish caught with simple improvised equipment. (No hunting and fishing licenses would be needed if you are so far off the beaten path that there is no one around to see you.) Energy needs would be minimal: a little Coleman gasoline for a cook stove perhaps, some candles and a small battery operated flashlight for light, but you would rely mainly on the sun and moon for lighting and adapt your daily schedule to natural light rather than try to turn night into day. Firewood gathered at each bivouac would supplement purchased energy supplies. Personal protection in this lifestyle would mainly depend on evasion and escape, though it would be useful to develop competence in one or more martial arts, and you might carry one or two carefully chosen, small and light pieces of defensive equipment.

The major items of equipment you will need on a long term walking tour are: good hiking boots, a light and roomy top quality backpacking tent, sleeping bag and a roll of plastic foam for a mattress, aluminum cookware and a small backpacking stove, and an aluminum frame backpack to carry everything in. In addition, you will be carrying food, clothing and personal gear. Since the initial outfitting would be your only major expense, it would not be wise to cut corners on these major pieces of equipment. Look for the highest quality in terms of function and durability.

Although your cash requirements would be quite low in this lifestyle, you would still need some cash, and you would not be holding down a normal job while travelling around this way. So where would your money come from? Here are a few ideas. One is that you could save up before embarking on this way of life, by working at normal employment, but spending as little of it as possible and saving the rest. If you start out with a modest stake, you could probably get along for many years in this lifestyle without needing any additional income. But if you would like to earn some continuing income, you need to look for location independent ways to make money. Some that come to mind are these: Make certain small craft items along the trail, say small wood carvings, or macrame, etc., and sell them at craft fairs or flea markets along the way. Or you might become an author. Carry writing materials and let the peace and tranquility of the natural surroundings inspire your creative expression. Or carry a camera and become a nature photographer. Another idea is to keep alert to employment opportunities along the way and pick up odd jobs whenever you come into contact with others. Of necessity, this will blow your cover as a "vacationer", but if you are discreet and reveal your desire for work only after feeling out your prospective employer, your problems should be minimal.

As a foot nomad, you can stay as well hidden as you like. Most of the population of this continent lives on a small percentage of the land. The rest is yours to use if you care to. If you enjoy your solitude, it would be best to stay away from the most popular National Parks, and other wilderness areas that attract huge crowds. A backpacker appears to be no threat to anyone, and he doesn't appear to have anything of much value. So he inspires neither enmity nor covetousness in the people who see him. You might run into an occasional forest ranger in the wilderness, but he will see you as just one of the millions of vacationing hikers and not really notice you. If you ever are stopped and questioned by The Man, you should have no problems provided you are prepared with good looking identification, a little cash, and a glib story about where you live and work (which should always be far away from wherever you are at that time). There is no need to mention that your "home address" is a mail drop at a friend's house, or that your have been "on vacation" for several years. You can't completely avoid being seen, but if you take care to look and sound like any of the millions of vacationing backpackers, that is what you will be taken for, and no one will suspect any different unless you tell them -- or unless you are careless enough to hang around one area for too many weeks.

There are a couple of problems with the foot nomad lifestyle that you might wonder about. Like: how would you deal with cold or rainy weather? Perhaps the best idea is to travel with the seasons, spend winter in the south, summer in the north. If you find yourself too far north with winter coming on, it would be a simple matter to take a bus, train, or plane -- or hitchhike or hop a freight -- and make a quick change of venue to a far off destination. Or you might come upon an unused cabin or a ghost town that you know will be snowed in all winter, and stock that up to be your winter quarters.

Another question that may occur to you is: what would you do with all your stuff, since a walker can carry only the bare essentials. A lot of your present possessions, like furniture, you just will not need. You can sell them, or give them away. Turn them into cash which is a lot more portable, as it can be put into banks, or used to buy gold coins which you can bury in secret places. For the rest, those prized possessions that you can't bear to part with, make a deal with a friend or relative to use some storage space in their attic or basement. Or you can set up caches at various places, underground, in caves, or whatever. In any case, you will probably find that your attachment to these possessions grows weaker as time passes. In a year or two you may find that you can now chuck out most of these stored items, as you come to enjoy your new freedom of not being weighted down with all this useless stuff.

For more information, see:

THE NEW COMPLETE WALKER, by Colin Fletcher. A.A. Knopf, New York. *Loaded with technical information, comprehensive detail. Go anywhere, live anywhere, comfortably and sensibly.*

CAMP AND TRAIL METHODS, by E. Kreps. A.R. Harding, Publisher, Columbus, Ohio, 1950. *A classic guide to outdoor living, includes: selecting a camp outfit, clothing, cooking utensils, beds and bedding, firearms, and lots more.*

GEOLOGICAL SURVEY MAPS. *These topographical maps prepared by the US Government are incredibly detailed, showing everything right down to foot trails and individual buildings. Write for index maps to the states you are interested in to: Map Information Service, US Geological Survey, Department of the Interior, Washington, DC 20240.*

Other maps and backpacking and hiking information are available from these other Government agencies:

National Park Service, Interior Building, Washington, DC 20240.

US Forest Service, 1318 N Chambliss St, Alexandria, VA 22312.

US Bureau of Land Management, C Street, Washington, DC 20240.

WINTER HIKING AND CAMPING, by John A. Danielson. Adirondack Mountain Club, Glens Falls, NY, 1972. *A basic handbook for planning excursions into the wilderness during winter. Covers the human body's response to cold, clothing, equipment, food, travel by various means, first aid, survival and rescue.*

BUSHCRAFT, by Richard Graves. Schocken Books, New York, 1975.

SURVIVAL, EVASION AND ESCAPE. Superintendent of Documents, Government Printing Office, Washington, DC 20402.

LIVING LIKE INDIANS, by A.A. McFarlan. Bonanza Press, Santa Cruz, California.

BACKPACKING ONE STEP AT A TIME, by Harvey Manning. Seattle, REI Press, 1972.

VAGABONDING IN AMERICA, by Ed Buryn. Random House, 1973.

HITCH HIKER'S FIELD MANUAL, by Paul DiMaggio. Mac-Millan, New York, 1973.

SNOW CAMPING AND MOUNTAINEERING, by Edward A. Rossit. Funk and Wagnalls, New York, 1970.

CHAPTER 11
LIVE AS A BICYCLE NOMAD

If you want to travel somewhat faster and in more comfort than on foot, and also to carry more weight than a backpacker can, consider a bicycle. The main disadvantage is that you won't be able to explore those rugged mountain trails on a bicycle. A bike needs pavement, or at least well graded dirt roads or trails, with not too many logs or rocks blocking the way. A modern bicycle is a marvelous machine. It actually requires less energy to travel a mile by bike than by any other means, including walking! Bicycle touring is pleasant and good for your health. And bicycle nomadism won't break anyone's budget. You can buy a top quality used bicycle for about $100, and bike repairs will be a minor expense. Traffic cops tend to ignore bicyclists, unless you do something really hazardous in traffic. Drivers of motor vehicles sometimes give bikes a hard time, so it is best to stay on the back roads, away from heavy traffic. You will want to get away from those exhaust fumes anyway. And some dogs think it is great fun to chase bicycles, but a spray of "Halt" or some similar chemical repellant on his nose will quickly change his mind. Bicycle touring is a popular sport all over the world, so a permanent bicycle nomad would be effectively invisible anywhere, just one more face in the crowd.

For more Information, see:

FREEWHEELING, by Ray Bridge. $3.95 plus 25¢ postage from Touring Cyclist Shop, PO Box 4009, Boulder, CO 80302. *The first complete book on bicycle camping.*

ANYBODY'S BIKE BOOK, by Tom Cuthbertson. Ten Speed Press, Berkeley, California, 1971. *East-to-follow instructions on bike repairing, also available from Touring Cyclist Shop for $3.95 plus 25¢ postage.*

RICHARD'S BICYCLE BOOK, by Richard Ballantine. *Tells all about bike types and structure, and how to buy, maintain, ride, and tour with one.*

THE AMERICAN BIKING ATLAS AND TOURING GUIDE, by Sue Browder. Workman Publishing Company, New York, 1974. *Describes 150 bike tours on quiet, scenic back roads through-out North America, in all kinds of regions: mountains, sea-*

shores, deserts, forests, swamps, prairies. Tells what each area is like: weather, people, plants, wildlife, road conditions, local bike shops, campsites.

CHAPTER 12
LIVE AS A CANOE NOMAD

The earliest European explorers of North America learned to make birchbark canoes from the Eastern woodland Indians and they used these marvelous vessels to explore the unknown continent. These days, canoeing is a popular sport. Canoeing is great fun and it turns every river and stream and lake into a highway to adventure. Canoes are light enough to be carried (portaged) around impassible stretches of water, or from one waterway to another.

This is another case where one can adopt the sportsman's technology as the basis for a nomadic way of life. Modern canoes can be made from several materials, ranging from the birchbark used by the Indians to aluminum or plastics. They come in a variety of sizes suitable for different numbers of passengers and various amounts of cargo. Canoes are light, silent, and cheap to buy and operate. Their shallow draft allows you to navigate quite small waterways and yet you can use them on the largest lakes, provided you stay close to shore for safety's sake. But some have even used canoes on the open ocean. Eskimoes use the kayak, which is a covered canoe, on the Arctic Ocean. And Polynesian adventurers travelled across thousands of miles of the Pacific Ocean in outrigger canoes.

A canoe nomad would have virtually no adverse impact on the environment. And canoe travel keeps you entirely off roads where you might meet the kind of people you would rather avoid. A canoe nomad would use basically the same kind of equipment as is used in bicycle touring or backpacking. A canoe could carry more weight, but, since all cargo would have to be backpacked over portages, excess weight should be avoided.

For more information, see:

POLE, PADDLE AND PORTAGE, by Bill Riviere. Little, Brown and Company, Boston, 1969. *A complete guide to canoeing, including: selecting a canoe, planning a canoe trip, equipment, handling a canoe, repairs, etc. Contains a chapter describing navigable streams in most states in the USA.*

If you get down their way, you might want to visit Ohio Canoe

Adventures, 5128 Colorado Ave, Sheffield Lake, OH 41054. *They stock over 10,000 hiking and canoeing guides in their shop.*

"The Endless Vacation or How To Live Very Well...On Practically Nothing", by Ida Little, in THE MOTHER EARTH NEWS No. 43, January 1977. *Tells about a couple who have been living for three years as canoe nomads in the Bahamas, open ocean island hopping in a canoe.*

CHAPTER 13

LIVE AS A HORSE NOMAD

In his book PRIVACY, author Bill Kaysing tells about meeting, even in this modern age, a genuine saddle tramp. He says: "This man, lean and taciturn, was riding a good looking Appaloosa and towing a pack animal loaded with all his worldly goods. This 20th Century cowboy had everything you'd expect, including a six gun and a .44 Winchester. He said he was heading for the upper Sierras, where he heard there was some ranch work."

This suggests a really attractive way of life for a person who likes horses and the out-of-doors. With a horse and pack animal you could carry more gear than you ever could in a backpack, and with less effort. You could get into places no wheeled vehicle could go. Probably no one would bother you, since you would project such a peaceful and harmless appearance. Moreover, you would spend most of your time on trails and obscure back roads, out of sight, out of mind. And since horses don't burn gasoline, you would be free from the price manipulations of the oil barons.

For a more detailed look at what life is like among a band of present day horse nomads, we have this report from writer Eldorado on "Horse Nomads In Present Day California", which first appeared in VONULIFE 73.

"We are horse nomads. Our ideal has been to combine the natural territorial range of the horse (about 100 miles in diameter) and its defense mechanism of fast flight over long distances to new grounds with the needs of people functioning as nomadic gatherers operating on a subsistence level. Recreational and profitable uses of the horses are fringe benefits.

"We dwell at several seasonal bases and a larger number of very temporary squat spots in an area of California having a great diversity of climate and elevation. Although containing areas of heavy population density, about 90% of our grounds are uninhabited. We are exploring other areas, about 100 miles apart center to center, which form links in a chain, and provide stations in an underground railroad allowing us to move people and things really long distances in rather short times.

"Moving through 'public lands' has never been a big problem; perhaps in part due to our taking on protective coloration as needed and the ability to present plausible explanations. There seems to be a tendency to accept a small group of people on horseback as having some reason for being wherever they are found: bird watchers, horse people, hunters, etc. Long stays are on private property belonging to friendly owners. We do encamp for long periods on one spot. However, every effort is made to keep ourselves in a state of readiness for movement on very short notice. We can split and function as sub groups or individuals and move on to known areas where supplies are already stashed. We can move hundreds of pounds of goodies if need be, and this can be an advantage over foot people, but horses require their own logistics. Everything has its compensations.

"We are a gregarious gang and like company. We need not conceal our camps too carefully because we can scramble and be many miles away by the next morning. There is a certain strength in numbers -- and a lot of fun. About 12 seems to be comfortable, but 20 or more would be a mob scene. We have some big tents and other gear suitable for a group living quite sumptuously while gypsying. Each individual has personal and horse gear allowing him to survive indefinitely alone on the trail.

"We avoid group ownership. Each person owns their own horse, equipment, etc. Short term cooperative ventures, trade work and trade use deals are common. At times the entire group has been involved in profit making schemes. Discussion determines who is to do what and what goods and services are worth. That amount is paid to each participant. The initiators of such projects usually act as their managers. At the windup of the affair, no more organization is needed.

"In routine affairs we all act as teachers to one another (including children, who are considered as small sized people). Knowledge along with the persuasive powers and energies of each person carry a certain amount of authority. Additionally we have councils in which someone may be selected to perform a certain job such as negotiating with a land owner or taking some money we all throw in the hat and shopping for needed supplies. There is no central authority. In the event of a person so conducting himself as to be obnoxious to others or to jeopardize the basic objectives of the group we can ask him to leave, and if he won't, we will!

"We are very oriented to the idea of living naturally and close

91

to nature. We live differently and forsake old patterns. We intend not to be acted upon. Our survival demands exclusion of non-survival people. Boozers, dopers and those who haven't the determination to take care of themselves are not welcome. Most of us are into various physical-spiritual integration trips. Ages range from 2 to 50 with complete equality between men and women. Relationships are an individual matter. But unlimited loyalty is required of the person to this planet and of the individual to the group.

"The money needs within our system are very low. We demand a great deal from our horses in appearance, usefulness, and in their capability of moving us many miles quickly. It's best to allocate about $35 per month (1973 dollars) to each for its keep. Then swap, scrounge, and bargain for horse feed and supplies to cut this cost; and also, put the critter to work to earn his keep. We have rented out horses, packed stuff for people, plowed up garden plots, hired out to motion picutre companies, and dragged logs out of the woods to be cut for firewood.

"Don't expect horses to live off the land in most of the country. Grass, weeds, and such may serve as 'filler', but we always carry along or have stashed concentrated feeds such as pellets or grain. A few days supply can be carried as it is light and compact. Know your area and map out places where you can buy supplies. Locate short cuts, trails which may cross private lands, but where trespass is not involved. In most states the trespass laws do not preclude your travelling over private lands per se. Rather, trespass must involve you doing damage or intending to do damage by entering private property.

"The travelling horse as such has not been intentionally bred, nor has its equipment been commercially produced, in about 75 years. There is a vast amount of good horse information in books. Look into the recent interest in 'Endurance Competition' and what is being learned there. Avoid bum steers from 'cowboys', dealers, and the proponents of one breed or another. Manufacturers are keen on gulling you into buying images wrought from old movies, TV, rodeos, and other hokum, in the form of overweight saddles, clothes intended for saloon musicians, and gadgets. We have had to develop our own criteria drawing from several schools of thought. One general warning: Dismiss the Great American Wild West Tradition! It has no relevancy. I will illustrate some tips in the following story:

"Some of us took a 30 mile trip down a desert valley to a new canyon-mouth camp site to check it out. It was arranged that an 'outsider' friend would meet us there for a visit, leaving from a different starting point and going by another route. Friend's short legged horse walks about 4½ miles per hour. It could trot at perhaps 7½ miles per hour, but neither the horse's conformation, friend's ability, nor the saddle he uses, encourages much of that. He claims his big saddle horn is 'good for roping steers'. What steers? He settles for a bone jarring jog exhausting to both horse and rider. Both his route and ours cross a BLM fence which he detours adding an hour to his trip, but not accounting for his additional three hours later arrival in sore condition.

"Ours was a different sort of trip, interrupted by picnic and skinny dipping at a spring, rest stops, investigating the candy potential of some cactus we found and goofing around. Our tall 'giraffes' walk easily at over 6 miles per hour as they were chosen for that ability. We can trot on smooth level stretches getting maximum mileage for effort expended. We get off to walk several times -- which we can do as our feet are not crammed into point-toed high-heeled boots suited to a Tijuana cab driver. And about that BLM fence: some bedding was draped over it (an old military trick for going over entanglements) and we just jumped over it."

For more information, see:

HORSES, THEIR SELECTION, CARE AND HANDLING, by Margaret C. Self. A.S. Barnes and Co., Box 421, Cranbury, NJ 08512. *A long established classic, covering selection of the horse, equipment, general care, handling, first aid.*

HORSES, HITCHES AND ROCKY TRAILS, by Joe Back. Swallow Press, 1139 S Wabash Av, Chicago, IL 60605. *Author is an experienced packer.*

"Mule Train Nomads: A Message From The Wilderness" by Connie Hawthorne, in THE MOTHER EARTH NEWS No 58, July 1979. *Relates the story of a family who live roaming the Arizona wilderness with five mules and a goat.*

CHAPTER 14

LIVE AS A MOTORCYCLE NOMAD

If you would like to travel faster and farther than you can go on foot or by bicycle or other non-motorized means, and yet not lay out the cash it would take to operate a large camper, then motorcycle camping might just fill the bill. Those who have tried it know that roaring down the highway on a hot "bike" is great fun. And a two wheeled vehicle will take you off the road into places where nothing with four wheels could ever go. In many places it is easy to run your bike off the road and stash it in some bushes to get it completely out of sight. The original cost, and fuel and repair bills are much less than the going rate for any four wheeled castle. And yet you can carry a lot more weight than you could on a bicycle or with a backpack.

But a motorcycle does have some disadvantages. It is a lot more visible than non-motorized means of travel, and bikers are seen as threatening by many people, which can lead to hostility. You can mitigate this somewhat by keeping your appearance as neat and respectable as possible. Fade into the crowd and cultivate a low profile. Also, spills are common on a bike; it is more dangerous than most other vehicles. So it is wise to wear adequately heavy clothing: boots, tough jeans and jacket, gloves, helmet and goggles. Warm clothing is a necessity when travelling in cold weather. And a windshield will cut the chilling wind and keep you warmer, as well as deflect stones and water tossed by the vehicle in front of you. A sturdy luggage rack will let you easily carry your camping gear. And there is even room for a passenger on a large motorcycle.

For more information, see:

THE COMPLETE MOTORCYCLE NOMAD, by Roger Lovin. *Guide to low cost motorcycle touring, how to choose a bike, what kind of gear you will need, how to survive on the road.*

THE BEGINNER'S GUIDE TO MOTORCYCLING, by Bill Kaysing. Frederick Fell, 386 Park Av S, New York,NY 10016.

NOMAD CYCLE

(This is a compromise between an off-road and a touring bike, based on a 600 cc four-stroke Kawaski.)

The trailer is low for the best stability and contains the necessities for setting up a base camp. This frees the bike for more ambitious off-road riding.

1. Pop-up tent
2. Solar shower
3. Washbasin
4. Camp stove
5. Water tank
6. Camo cover for bike

CHAPTER 15

LIVE IN A CAMPER OR MOTOR HOME

You can enjoy the highest level of comfort while still following a nomadic lifestyle by living in a four wheeled motorized vehicle. A large number of people -- retired couples, young families, and all ages in between -- already live this way. You can choose from a wide variety of equipment over a large price range. At the top of the line, ten grand or more will buy you a self-contained motor home as well-equipped as a luxury apartment. Moving down the line, you can choose from converted buses, chasis-mounted campers, vans, slide-in campers mounted in pickups, down to worn-out delivery trucks. Some people even live in cars. If you have very little cash to start with, you can throw a mattress and some camping gear into an old vehicle of some sort and you're on the road. Later, as finances permit, you can upgrade your lifestyle to whatever level you desire.

There are various places you can park your home ranging from hidden spots in the wilderness, to established campsites, to city streets and parking lots, or a friend's driveway. A camper is an expensive means of transportation and is not really suitable for one who is constantly travelling. A better way to use it is for mainly seasonal migration and infrequent trips.

The essential details of one version of this lifestyle, which is called "land mobile nomadism", has been described in this way by one proponent:

"The land mobile nomad family (say, two adults and three children) lives in two campers. They have scouted and prepared a number of "squat-spots" at different locations but all on uninhabited non-privately-owned land. The family as a whole moves from squat-spot to squat-spot; the pattern of movement is somewhat seasonal. When funds are needed, one parent commutes weekly to the city utilizing the smaller camper for transportation and city housing. The other parent and children live in the larger camper which remains at the squat-spot, which is where the children are educated. For auxiliary storage they have caches and rented space outside the city. They do some foraging but, partly because of the easy proximity of city work and stores, they rely mainly on purchased supplies. Protection is through concealment while at the squat-spot, mobility when

MOBILE HOME/CAMPER

(NOTE: Large mobile homes are often custom-built; the layout shown here is by no means the only one! This is a moderately sized 24-foot model.)

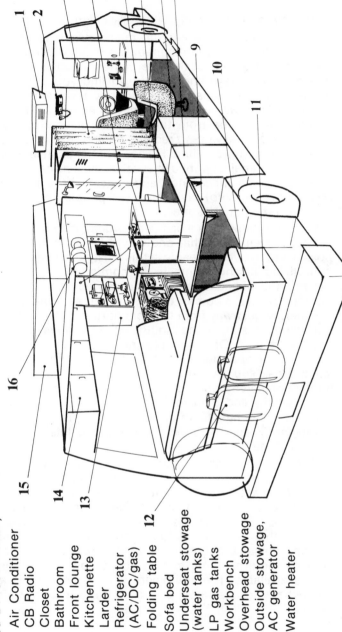

1. Air Conditioner
2. CB Radio
3. Closet
4. Bathroom
5. Front lounge
6. Kitchenette
7. Larder
8. Refrigerator (AC/DC/gas)
9. Folding table
10. Sofa bed
11. Underseat stowage (water tanks)
12. LP gas tanks
13. Workbench
14. Overhead stowage
15. Outside stowage, AC generator
16. Water heater

disturbed, and anonymity while travelling or in the city."

For the freedom seeker the main advantage of living in a camper is that the government exerts much control over people by taking advantage of their permanent residence on their real estate. They always know where to find you. If you own real estate, government can control you by threatening to seize it, and there is no way you can effectively defend it. The motorized nomad can escape from these points of control. By moving frequently and leaving no records behind (pay bills in cash), he makes himself hard to find. He has a better chance of defending his property against public thieves because he can drive it away, then change its appearance, and conceal it. As the song *(Goin' Mobile, by The Who)* says about van people: "Watch the police and the tax man miss me".

Yet at the same time a camper resident, if he wishes, can have all the conveniences that one would find in a fixed home. It is possible to live very cheaply in this lifestyle. Or you can upgrade your living arrangements to as comfortable a level as your desires and finances permit. You can enjoy travelling to visit different places. You can travel with the seasons to avoid bad weather, to get away from the cold northern winter, to avoid the hurricane season in the Southeast, to always be where the weather is best. Or you could travel to where there are more employment opportunities, instead of job hunting in only one small area. You can spend most of your time in unspoiled, lightly populated wilderness areas if you like, and yet still live in the city now and then for convenient shopping and to enjoy what city life has to offer. Or, if you prefer, you can live permanently on city streets and parking lots, as many have already done.

This way of life is not an untried scheme that you would have to pioneer from scratch. So many are doing it that even the *Wall Street Journal* took notice of it in a front page article devoted to the subject on August 21, 1978 ("The Nomads: To Thousands in US, Home, Sweet Home Is A Place With Wheels"). They estimate that there are untold thousands of people who have become nomads, although no one knows for sure how many nomads there are. Information about how to live this way is readily available. The equipment you would need is available everywhere at reasonable prices. In this approach to freedom, the path has already been broken before you. All that one needs is the resolve to follow it.

For more information, see:

HOME IS WHERE YOU PARK IT, by Kay Peterson. Follet Publishing Company, Chicago, 1977. *A complete guide to RV living as a lifestyle, covering both practical and psychological aspects, such as equipment, employment, parking problems, schooling for children, emergencies, leaving friends, living in confined quarters, and more.*

ROLL YOUR OWN, The Complete Guide To Living In A Truck, Bus, Van, Or Camper, by Jodi Pallidini and Beverly Dubin. MacMillan Publishing Co, New York, 1974. *This is an illustrated handbook most useful for its many pictures of the far-out and funky vehicles that counter-culture people are living in. Also covers numerous details of setting up a camper and living in it including storage, beds, stoves, water, lighting, refrigeration, etc.*

THE COMPLETE BOOK OF MOTOR CAMPING, by Lyle Kenyon Engle. Arco Books,New York, 1971.

ALL ABOUT PICKUP CAMPERS, VAN CONVERSIONS AND MOTOR HOMES, by John Gartner. Trail-R-Club of America, Santa Monica, 1969.

LIVING ON WHEELS, by Richard Wolters. E.P. Dutton and Co, New York, 1973.

"Trailer Life" (magazine), 29901 Agoura Road, Agoura, CA 91301. $1.50 per issue; subscription $8.50 per year.

"Woodall's Trailer and RV Travel" (magazine), 10 Caravan Court, Marion, OH 43302. Monthly, $9.50 per year.

CHAPTER 16
LIVE IN AN AIRSHIP

In one part of the book GULLIVER'S TRAVELS, the author weaves a fantasy about a visit to a mythical city that floats in the sky. It now appears that the idea may not be so far from reality after all. Today we could build, not an entire city that floats in the sky, but at least a sky home, a habitat which would be the permanent residence of a family or small group of people. Such a habitat would take the form of a blimp, an airship, a lighter-than-air vehicle.

The key fact which makes it possible to conceive of an airship as a permanent home is this: an airship that uses helium as its lifting gas doesn't require fuel to remain airborne. Thus an airship can be compared to a luxury yacht, which also can be (and often is) used as a permanent home. But the airship, this yacht that sails in the sky, is superior to the water borne vessel in that the airship can travel anywhere on Earth, over land or sea, and from the tropics to the poles.

The average person may think of the airship as a device whose day is over, one that was tried and has been proved unsafe. But, in fact, new developments in materials, electronics, and engineering since the heyday of the rigid airships in the 1930's, and even since the last large scale use of non-rigid blimps in the 1950's, point to an almost inevitable second coming of the airship. New technology provides solutions to most of the problems encountered by the old airships. The modern airship would be inflated with nonflammable helium or hot air instead of the dangerous hydrogen used in the German airships of the 1930's. The structure now would be made of stronger, lighter materials like titanium or fiberglass, instead of aluminum. The envelope and gas cells would be made of new plastics, perhaps of kevlar which is five times stronger than steel, yet has half the weight of nylon, instead of the weak and leaky doped cotton fabric used in the 1930's. Electronic controls would allow one person to control the whole ship, and eliminate the need for a large crew stationed at every engine and control surface. These and other innovations would make the modern airship safe and reliable, as far advanced from the airships of the past as a modern luxury recreational vehicle is from a Model T

Ford.

Let's consider how a modern airship could be used as a home for living free. The airship would stay afloat most of the time above international waters, perhaps over the Pacific Ocean. It might travel leisurely in a large circular route. Starting near the west coast of North America, the airship would fly south under power until it reached the region of the southeast trade winds. Then it would conserve fuel by free ballooning before the wind across the Pacific. Nearing Asia, it would use its engines again to fly north until it reached the prevailing westerly winds above the equator. Then the engines would be shut down again and the sky home would drift before the wind back to North America, where the circle would begin again.

An airship flying this route would use minimal fuel. It would always stay in subtropical or warmer regions, mostly beyond government authority over international waters. It could stop at uninhabited Pacific islands for a change of scene and to gather food and water. And it could stop at populated places to buy fuel and to enjoy other amenities of civilization. Of course, side trips could be made to any part of the world if desired. An airship can easily fly around the world as the Graf Zeppelin did in 1929. Or it could visit polar regions, following the lead of the airships Norge, Italia, or Graf.

An airship could earn income by carrying freight or passengers, or by contracting to do other chores. Travelers who are more interested in travelling in comfort and style rather than speed would find an airship voyage even better than passage aboard an ocean liner. The economics of airship transport make it the ideal choice for the shipment of low density, high volume carge. And the airship is perfect for doing other jobs that require flying low or hovering -- for example aerial photography or surveying. It is much cheaper and has less vibration than a helocopter, which is the only other option for such tasks. An airship could also be used to exploit natural resources found in uninhabited or isolated places. It could land on small islands that are almost inaccessible to boats because they lack good harbors, and take aboard bulky cargoes such as metallic ores, or lumber, etc. and transport them at low cost to distant markets for sale. Since an airship can take off and land straight up and down, it needs no prepared runway. Any unobstructed flat area like a meadow or beach would serve. An airship could even visit

Arctic or sub-Antarctic islands that are hard to get to by water, due to turbulent and often ice-clogged seas.

A modern airship might include certain innovative features such as these: it could use a dual gas system to provide lift, consisting of helium cells surrounded by hot air cells. A similar system was used in the balloon that made the first successful crossing of the Atlantic by balloon recently. The expensive helium, which provides greater lift, would balance most of the empty weight of the ship, but it would be vented off only in an emergency. The hot air could be vented as needed to allow for ascent and descent. While burning a fuel would provide much of the hot air used for lift, and would provide the quick response needed for control, solar energy could be used on sunny days to heat air and thus reduce the fuel requirement. Someday it might even be possible to use solar energy, converted into electricity in photo-voltaic cells, as a source of power for the airship. The solar energy would run electric motors that drive propellers to power the airship. Two graduate students at Cal Tech have built a model solar powered airship using this idea. Right now solar cells are too expensive for large scale use, but their cost is coming down steadily. The solar powered airship would need fuel-burning generators as backup for travel on cloudy days and at night. This use of solar energy would greatly reduce the airship's fuel expense.

Another innovation would be to equip the airship so that it would seldom have to land. Freight, supplies, and passengers could be lifted up to the airborne ship, or be taken down by helicopter. Members of the crew could come and go via individual powered hang gliders. But ground handling techniques have been developed to the point where only a few persons, using a portable mooring mast, could speedily land or launch an airship.

Perhaps an airship could even land and launch itself, following this scenario: As the airship approaches its destination, which might be an uninhabited island, a landing site would be selected from the air. This could be a meadow or any other area clear of tall vegetation and obstructions. The ground crew would descend to the field from the airship using powered hang gliders. A portable mooring mast carried aboard the airship would be lowered to the ground. The ground crew would set up and secure the mast and bring the airship in for a secure landing. Launching would proceed in reverse. The airship would be separated from the mast and would lift off straight up. The ground crew would disassemble the mooring mast and it would be lifted up by cables into the airship hovering overhead. Then the ground crew would fly up to rejoin the airship using the engines in their hang gliders.

Briefly, let me summarize some other features of this airborne, free roaming lifestyle:

Food would have to be imported, but it could be gathered, hunted, farmed, or fished for in uninhabited places. Pure water would have to be resupplied the same way. Or rain could be caught, or sea water could be taken up during a low hover and purified by distilling, perhaps in a solar still. Solar energy would be available in the airship, but imports of hydrocarbon fuels would be the main energy source. Security would be poor as a result of an airship being large, visible, and slow, but it might not be easy to find when it is somewhere over the vast ocean. It couldn't be concealed in the air, but it could be tucked away under cover while landed on an uninhabited island.

There is no upper limit to the size of the living space that could be made available in an airship, but the larger the size, the more it would cost. And the cost of the vehicle required to set up this lifestyle would be in the high range even for the smallest feasible ship. The inhabitants of the airship could enjoy any climate depending on where it travels, from the tropics to the poles. The airship could stay mostly in minimally polluted areas over oceans or over polar regions and avoid the greater pollution over populated lands or the much greater pollution of urban areas. The airship could either avoid populated areas or spend as much time in populated places as desired. A certain minimum of technology would be required to make this lifestyle possible, so it couldn't be very primitive. At the other extreme, the sky is the limit, for life aboard an airship could be as opulent and splendid as money could provide.

For more information, see:

AIRSHIPS FOR THE FUTURE, by William J. White. Sterling Publishing Company, New York, 1978. *Good description of the principles of lighter-than-air flight, the present state of the art, and future prospects.*

WHY HAS AMERICA NO RIGID AIRSHIPS? by P.W. Litchfield and Hugh Allen. Originally written in 1945, and revised in 1976. 7 C's Press, Inc., PO Box 57, Riverside, CT 06878. *An excellent book, whose most interesting feature is the accounting for the several disasters that marred the early history of the airship.*

THE GREAT DIRIGIBLES, THEIR TRIUMPHS AND DIS—ASTERS, by John Toland. Dover Publications, New York, 1972. *History of the great airships.*

"Buoyant Flight, The Bulletin of the Lighter-Than-Air Society", 1800 Triplett Blvd, Akron, OH 44306. *Newsletter. The Society also sells many books about airships. Associate membership is $5 per year.*

"Advanced Lighter Than Air Review", 1067 National Press Bldg, Washington, DC 20045. *A recently started newsletter that reports the latest developments in the LTA field.*

"Inside The Control Car", 910 Sherwood Lake Drive No. 3B, Schererville, IN 46375. *A newsletter written by and for LTA enthusiasts with mostly historical articles.*

Association of Balloon and Airship Constructors, PO Box 7, Rosemead, CA 91770. *Publishes a quarterly journal AERO-STATION, and a quarterly newsletter. They have a variety of LTA books and booklets for sale. Associate membership is $10 per year.*

PART IV
LIVE IN OTHER UNUSUAL PLACES

CHAPTER 17
LIVE IN A SECRET CELLAR

You can live free in your domestic life by developing your real home in a secret cellar that you build under your apparent residence. The cellar could be located under an existing building in the city or out in the country. Entrance to the secret cellar would be through that building via a hidden door. You would actually live in this secret place, spending most of your at-home time there, and sleeping there. You might maintain a phony residence upstairs as a cover, but you wouldn't leave any important possessions up there, and you would spend little time there. Having a secret home like this won't make you any freer when you are out on the street, but it will give you much more freedom, security, and peace of mind during that part of your life that you spend at home.

The advantages of living in such a secret space are that your valuables would be almost totally protected from thieves, including burglars, looters during riots, or taxmen. If you earn your living on the free market, and don't tell the tax boys about some of your income, then it would be wise not to appear very wealthy. In a secret cellar home you could surround yourself with expensive electronic equipment, oriental carpets, fine wines, or whatever you prefer, and no one will know about it unless you tell them.

Another benefit is that, if properly insulated, an underground living space is energy efficient, cheap to heat and cool. And the risk of fire is normally much less than in a typical wooden crackerbox house. Also, it is quiet underground. Those tons of earth next to the walls block out virtually all surface noise. This means you could buy a house next to an airport or a superhighway which is low priced due to the noise, and then build a secret cellar there, where you won't hear the noise at all.

You would be physically safe in your secret underground home. No burglar or rapist will break in during the night to do you harm. There have been cases of people shot in their homes by bullets fired through a window or through a wall. You could forget about that. And police have been known to kick in a door in the middle of the night. Sometimes they even break into the wrong house and shoot perfectly innocent people. You can sleep soundly in a secret cellar, knowing that the police won't even find your real door. If they do break in upstair, they will find no one at home. No cop would ever think of looking for a hidden door to your real home somewhere down below. And if you have done a good job, they won't find the door even if they look for it. It would be a good idea to build in some devices that will let you monitor what is happening upstairs, and see if the coast is clear before you leave your secret place. At least you can bug the upstairs so you can hear what is going on.

Lastly, many people will find that having a secret place and a secret life is great fun. You will find yourself smiling a lot, every time you think about what you alone know. And you will feel a great satisfaction when you hear others worry out loud about burglaries, murder and mayhem, which you are completely immune to in your home.

A secret cellar can be developed in a rural or an urban setting. Out in the country you might build under a barn, or a shack, or in a ghost town. During the excavation you will have to hide the evidence of the digging, unless you can make it look like some other reasonable activity. If you don't want it to become known that anyone is living there, you'll have to be careful not to be seen coming and going from your cover building. Also, you should be careful not to make any trails. It would be easier if you could let it be known that you live there, and just hide how well you live. Then you could come and go freely; just avoid dressing too well. Don't do much to improve the appearance of the shack or old farmhouse that sits on top of your secret place. Put most of your energy into your real home, which is secure from all aggressors.

But this secret cellar strategy really comes into its own in a city residence. In the city it would be virtually impossible to prevent your neighbors seeing your coming and going. So it would be best to make it look like you live upstairs. Keep your curtains closed but turn lights on and off upstairs at appropriate times while you are home in the evenings. Make it look like your income is only average or below average. Don't bother anybody. Don't let it look like you have much of value that anybody would want. In order to have the time and secure possession of the property to develop your secret cellar, you would probably have to own the house. Or you might manage to rent on a long term lease, preferably from someone you can trust not to ask you to move. It would be very useful if the house you selected had an attached garage. This would let you load or unload your vehicle with the garage door closed. Thus you could take out the dirt you excavate or bring in valuables, without your nosy neighbors knowing about it. Furnish your upstairs space with used furniture of no value. Keep it stocked with all the necessities that would normally be found there. And spend a few minutes now and then keeping the place looking like it was lived in, but don't keep anything really valuable up there. If possible, don't let anyone know about your secret cellar. Socialize with friends at their homes, or upstairs at your house if necessary. If you never reveal to anyone your real home downstairs, there is no way they can deliberately or inadvertently spill the beans on you.

With this strategy you sacrifice mobility. Living in a secret cellar, there is no possibility of making a quick getaway and taking all your valuables with you. And a secret cellar would represent a large investment of time and money and effort which you might be reluctant to abandon. Of course, you could combine a secret cellar with other strategies. For example, you could also keep a well-stocked camper on hand for emergency use, or you could even live a nomadic life most of the time and use the secret cellar as an occasionally visited home base.

A secret cellar would be constructed in a built-up area which is under the control of some government, so it would be more vulnerable than a lifestyle developed beyond government jurisdiction. A secret cellar would provide a small amount of living space, since every cubic foot would have to be excavated with a great deal of effort. Building a secret cellar would be costly, especially in terms of the time it takes. And you would have to do all the work yourself. Hiring the work done would make the existence of the cellar known, which would compromise your security and defeat your purpose. To lighten your workload, you should plan carefully and purchase all the materials, equipment, and appropriate tools that you need to make the job go faster and easier.

For more information, see:

UNDERGROUND DESIGNS, by Malcolm Wells. Box 1149, Brewster, MA 02631, 1977. *Contains mostly drawings of underground buildings (not hidden), but it also has much useful technical information about building underground (structural support, insulation, waterproofing, etc.).*

HOW TO HIDE ALMOST ANYTHING, by David Krotz. Morrow, New York, 1975. *This is mostly about building small, hidden cubbyholes to conceal your valuables, but it also provides some ideas about how to conceal the entrance to a larger living space.* THE STASH BOOK, by Peter Hjersman. And/Or Press, Berkeley, CA, 1978. *This is a survey of the joy of hiding, with a chapter on the art of hiding people, and fascinating hints about the "ninja", the fantastic secret agents of medieval Japan, as well as the abolitionist underground railroad, and the priest's holes used by persecuted Roman Catholics in Elizabethan England.*

CHAPTER 18
LIVE IN A GHOST TOWN

There are hundreds of abandoned ghost towns in the West. A freedom seeker could find a suitable ghost town with a building suitable for use as a home. He would leave the outside of it as it is for protective coloration, and fix up some rooms inside to live in.

The advantages of living in a ghost town are that most of them are far away from where many other people live. If you are willing to settle for something less than perfection, it would be easier than building completely from scratch because you can find structures still half standing to work with. And there are usually plenty of extra building materials nearby. Some places will have a developed water supply with a well or pipes in place. There would be no need to hide all signs of your habitation too well, since the changes you make can be made to blend in with the changes caused by the previous habitation. Old mining towns may still have some valuable ore in the claims, which might provide you with some income.

Finding a ghost town is easy. There are many guide books to ghost towns and old maps showing where they are. Many tourists visit ghost towns, but usually only the ones easiest to reach. So while looking for your special place, be a tourist, camera around your neck and all. Then if you run into anyone, it's no sweat. Once you find the place where you want to stay, you can shuck off the tourist garb.

When living in a ghost town, you could eat staple foods that can be stored for a long time that you bring in from outside, which you might supplement with foraged wild foods, as well as game that you get by hunting or trapping. If you grow food in a garden, that should be done away from where you live for security, and the garden might also be concealed or dispersed among a number of small plots. Energy sources appropriate to this lifestyle would be firewood that you gather and imports of hydrocarbon fuels, especially for cooking -- but you would want to avoid building smoky fires.

Security would be high in this lifestyle as a result of your distance away from where other people live (since the most suitable ghost towns would be found in wilderness areas), and as a result of concealment. While a ghost town habitat would not itself be moveable, this lifestyle could easily be combined with some form of nomadism. One could, for example, develop a number of ghost town habitats and travel from one to another, on a regular circuit. Then if any problem arose at the place where you are staying, you could slip away and go to another of your prepared hideouts.

These ghost towns are all within territory owned by some government, but the deeper wilderness places may not be very effectively controlled by the authorities. The size of the living space could be as large as you want to make it, but larger improved spaces may be less easy to conceal. The cost of setting up a ghost town home could be almost nothing, or it could be as much money as you want to spend. The more valuable the property you bring in, the better it should be concealed, to prevent it being ripped off -- especially if you expect to be away from your habitat for long periods of time. The income possibilities that exist in a place like this are the location-independent type of occupations that are also appropriate to nomadic lifestyles, as well as gathering wilderness products, trapping for furs, and exploiting mineral resources from old claims. In this ghost town lifestyle, you would be able to hide away and build up a stash of a saleable commodity until you have accumulated enough to make a trip to your buyer to sell your product worthwhile.

This lifestyle would tend to put you into places with a rugged climate, like mountains, north woods, and deserts. These wilderness areas tend to be low in population and less polluted than more built-up areas. The quality of the lifestyle this approach would offer would tend to be close to nature and rugged rather than genteel and luxurious. This lifestyle would give you easy access to the markets and amenities available in North America, while allowing you to maximize your freedom. This strategy would restrict the access to you of those forces that are detrimental to your welfare and happiness.

For more information, see:

NEVADA GHOST TOWN TRAILS, by A.L. Abbott. Gem Guides Book Co., Whittier, CA. 1973.

CALIFORNIA-NEVADA GHOST TOWN ATLAS, by Robert Neil Johnson. Cy Johnson and Son, Susanville, CA, 1974.

GHOST TOWNS AND MINING CAMPS OF CALIFORNIA, by Remi Nadeau. The Ward Ritchie Press, Los Angeles, 1972.
Many, many more guides to ghost towns are available -- one good source is Carson Enterprises, Inc., 801 Juniper Avenue, Boulder, CO 80302. Write for a complete catalog.

And you could do some **research in libraries**, looking through old books and maps that describe mining camps and boom towns of the last century. Also see old railroad maps. Compare with more modern maps. Towns that are shown on the old maps, but not on the more recent ones are what you are looking for.

CHAPTER 19
LIVE IN A CAVERN

There are several variations of the idea of living in a cavern or cave. Cave dwelling suggests the image of living near the mouth of a small underground opening. This would not offer many advantages if the cave were located near civilization, but a cave in a remote wilderness would be secure. Also, one located high up on an inaccessible cliff face, reached only by a ladder that could be pulled up behind you, like some ancient Indian cliff dwelling, would make a secure refuge.

Living in a cavern, on the other hand, suggests a huge underground space like, say, Carlsbad Caverns, where you could wall off a side chamber for your residence, or build a stone house. An abandoned mine could be used the same way. In a mine you would have to watch out for rotted, weak timbers that were used to shore up the roof. These should be replaced with stone or concrete for durability. Of course, you would want to leave the outside of the mine unimproved, to aid concealment.

Or, if you don't have a handy cavern or mine at hand, you could dig your own tunnel into soft rock, or even into loose dirt, provided that you shore up the roof as you go. Or you could use the cut and cover technique: dig out a hole, say 10 feet deep; build a roof over it a couple feet below the surface; and put the topsoil back over it to conceal it and blend it in with its surroundings. To complete the work, you will want to make a hidden entrance to your tunnel. You might hide a small opening behind some bushes in a thicket. Or make a perfectly visible door that doesn't look like a door. But don't try to make a copy of a natural object for a door, like an artificial tree stump. It would be extremely difficult to do that convincingly. A better idea would be to make an admittedly artificial object, which looks like it belongs where it is, and won't draw a second glance. For example, on a patio you might build a brick barbeque that swings aside to reveal a trap door.

All surface land is owned by some government. The advantage of underground space is that it is new land, often unknown and therefore unregulated and untaxed. Building codes can be ignored by those who build out of sight underground. Property taxes won't apply. Underground space, and all valuables placed there, can be as completely hidden as you like, to give you complete security against any ripoffs. A luxurious home developed in secret, underground, will not be seen by any taxmen who might inquire whether you paid taxes on all the income that went into building it.

Other advantages of living in a cavern are: there is no bad weather underground. The humidity doesn't vary much. The temperature remains constant throughout the year in most caves, near the average annual temperature for that geographic region. Cave rooms can be easily walled off to keep out undesireable men or beasts. An underground dwelling in the wilderness, or on undeveloped property, would allow you to use an exploit and enjoy the surface features while keeping your valuable property safe and hidden.

One problem with cavern living is that darkness is total, so you will need artificial light. But this shouldn't be any more of a problem than when working in a modern office with no windows. Artificial tunnels will need to be ventilated, but natural caverns usually have a sufficient infiltration of fresh air. However, don't make your home in an old coal mine, because these often fill with suffocating and explosive methane gas. Some people might find the total lack of natural light and the unchanging weather in a cavern disturbing and even unhealthy over a long period of time. But you would probably not be spending all of your time in a cavern home, any more than you now spend all of your time in the home where you presently live. No doubt you would want to come up sometimes to bask in the sunshine, or to feel the rain and wind on your face. Then later you would return to your cozy, secure retreat beneath the surface.

If you are not very familiar with caverns, you can learn more about them by visiting commercial caverns that have been developed to attract tourists. Many other caves are well known, even though not commercially exploited. Members of caving clubs (known as cavers or spelunkers) mount frequent expeditions to explore known caves. Following is a table of some of the caverns in North America.

Carlsbad Caverns ....**New Mexico**
Mammoth Cave ....**Kentucky**

Mark Twain Cave	Missouri
Endless Caverns	New Market, Virginia
Howe Caverns	New York
Fairy Cave	Missouri
Marengo Cave	Crawford County, Indiana
Niagra Caverns	Harmony, Minnesota
Luray Caverns	Virginia
Ice Mine	Coudersport, Pennsylvania
Ape Cave	Washington
Blow Out Cave	Texas
Wind Cave	South Dakota
Butter Cave	Washington
Cameron Cave	Missouri
Cave of the Catacombs	California
Cathedral Cave	Missouri
Crystal Caverns	Missouri
Cumberland Caverns	Tennessee
Eagle Cave	Wisconsin
Floyd Collins Crystal Cave	Kentucky
Fossil Mountain Ice Cave	Wyoming
Grand Caverns	Virginia
Gunther Mountain Cave	Alabama
Gypsum Cave	Nevada
Jacob's Cave	Missouri
Lone Hill Onyx Cave	Missouri
Massanutten Cavern	Virginia
Meat Cave	Washington
Miller's Cave	California
Cave of the Mounds	Wisconsin
Ney Cave	Texas
Potato Cave	Oregon
Railroad Cave	Missouri
Sea Lion Cave	Oregon
Shenandoah Caverns	Virginia
Tavern Cave	Missouri
Trillium Cave	Washington
Tunnel Cave	Missouri
Zell Cave	Missouri
Decorah Ice Cave	Decorah, Iowa

While we all know about ancient cave men, here are some more recent examples of people living in and using caves and tunnels:

In ancient Rome, burial galleries called catacombs were dug into the rock under the city. Early Christians, while they were being persecuted by the Roman government, used the catacombs for their meetings and ceremonies.

The sewers of Paris have often been used as hideouts by thieves and other Parisian criminals. In his novel *Les Miserables,* author Victor Hugo has his hero flee from the police through the sewers of Paris.

When the Warsaw Ghetto rose in revolt against Nazi persecution in 1944, the Jewish rebels occupied the city's sewers, and used them as their living quarters and base of operations.

At about the same time, over in the Pacific, Japanese troops used caves and tunnels and built underground fortifications on many Pacific islands such as Iwo Jima, from which they put up a fierce resistance, and forced the invading US forces to pay a high price in casualties to gain control of these islands.

A generation later, the Viet Cong spent thirty years constructing a tunnel system that stretched over 150 miles and used it as their base for their successful conquest of South Vietnam.

In a more peaceful vein, in the US southwest we find the ruins of Indian pueblos built high up on cliff faces. When these settlements were occupied in pre-Columbian days, the cliff dwellers gained access by using ladders which they pulled up behind them, thus making their homes inaccessible to invaders.

In central Anatolia, Turkey, lies another indigenous cave settlement that is still occupied. These are the Cones of Cappadocia, pinnacles of soft volcanic rock that have been hollowed out to make homes, shops, graneries, churches, etc. over a period of some 2,000 years.

And recently a reporter for the *New York Times* happened to discover a "steam pipe community" of street people living in the maze of tunnels that go down six levels underneath New York City's Park Avenue. There among the hissing steam pipes, several dozen people make their homes and manage to keep warm and out of sight beneath the bustling metropolis.

Let us look at some of the details of living in an underground place. Because there is no light to support growth, food would have to be mostly imported. But there are some exceptions. Mushrooms must be grown in the dark, but they do need some kind of composted manure as a growth medium. This could be made from bat guano, however, which is found in many caves. The bats themselves are small mammals which would probably make a satisfactory food. Livestock have been raised in caves for weeks at a time, and they apparently do all right in that environment. Hens will lay eggs in caves. Cows will probably give milk. Of course, livestock must be fed on feed brought in from outside. Sprouting of seeds requires no light and could be done underground. Yeast will grow without light, so fermentation processes are possible, including making cheeses and wine and beer.

In natural caverns, drinking water is often available -- in fact, entire rivers and lakes are found underground. Water would generally have to be brought into smaller caves and tunnels. But often they would be below the water source, which would make a gravity-powered water system possible.

Few sources of energy are available in caverns, so fuels would have to be imported. One exception is that in some cases water power might be available in underground rivers and water falls, and this could be harnessed in a small hydroelectric plant. Another possible energy resource lies in the bat guano found in bat caves. During both the American Revolutionary War and the Civil War, saltpeter was leached out of bat guano for use in making gunpowder. And the author of CAVERNS OF THE WORLD tells how in 1856 a hunter in Texas tried to smoke a bear out of a cave by building a bonfire at the cave entrance. Well, the cave had a large deposit of bat guano and when he lit the fire the guano gases exploded. The guano burned for two years at what is now known as Blow Out Cave. No trace of either hunter or bear was ever found. This suggests that bat guano could either be burned directly as a fuel or that it could be used as the raw material from which some other fuel, such as methane perhaps, could be made. Another idea is that if the cave or cavern is located in a remote area, above ground energy sources such as solar energy, wind power, or water power could be tapped and wires carrying the electricity generated could be run down into the underground home.

The size of the living space available in a natural cavern would probably be more than you could use. In the case of an artificial tunnel that you would build, though, space would be harder to come by since every cubic foot would require considerable work to excavate.

The cost of living in a cavern could be minimal. Just take in the camping gear that you need and set up your camp. Or you could spend much more and establish quite a luxurious abode.

Most ways of earning a living would be accessible to a cavern dweller. Any mail order business could be operated, provided you could get to a Post Office reasonably often. Handicrafts could be made in a cave home. In fact, there would be no size or weight limitations on the scale of your manufacturing endeavors in a large cavern. But both the raw materials coming in and the product going out would have to be reasonably easy to transport. You might even be able to commute to an ordinary job from a cave home, if it were located not too far from civilization. And a cavern might have valuable mineral deposits that could be sold. An abandoned mine would be an even more likely source of valuable deposits, either in the mine itself or overlooked in the previously worked tailings. Very often a mine that is no longer of commercial value has small mineral deposits remaining that would be enough to support one person or a family, especially if you don't need much income.

If you can be content in an environment with unchanging "weather", total darkness (except for what light you create), total silence (except for the sounds you make and perhaps the sound of running water), solitude (unless you bring in companions with you), and no burglars, muggers, taxmen, or other two-legged vermin to bother you -- if you can be content with these conditions, then there is no limit to what you can build, to the quality of the lifestyle you can create in a cavern or similar underground space.

For more Information, see:

CAVERNS OF THE WORLD, by Alonzo Pond. W.W. Norton and Co., New York, 1969. *A general introduction to caves.*

National Speleological Society, Cave Avenue, Huntsville, AL 35810. *Source of further information on conditions to be found in caves and cave exploring clubs.*

Miner's Catalog, Riggins, ID 83549. *A source for geological equipment and books on mining, minerals, ores, etc.*

CHAPTER 20

LIVE IN A DESERT

Throughout the world the deserts are growing larger as marginal lands dry up and become denuded of vegetation. Deserts already cover nearly 20% of the surface of the Earth. While this increasing desertification is a disaster for many people, for the freedom seeker it can also be seen as an opportunity. For as lands grow more barren, they become unpopulated -- deserted (which is what "desert" really means). While the world's population continues to increase, it is also becoming increasingly concentrated into urban areas, and the relatively empty lands are becoming still emptier. Already less than 4% of the world's population live in deserts. These deserts beckon to freedom lovers who want to avoid other people and governments who would impose a tyrannical rule over them.

Of course, if you hope to live in a place like a desert where others have not succeeded in surviving before, you must have a new idea -- you can't just repeat the same way of life that didn't work for others who have gone before you. But in some deserts that are not totally barren, a more traditional way of life may be possible. In the US southwest, you could perhaps live off the land as a nomad, leading a pack animal or two, looking like an old-time prospector. You might find a little "color" in your pan now and then, or locate some other mineral resources, to supply your modest cash needs. You would appear so harmless and picturesque that probably no one would bother you.

But if the idea of camping out all the time is not appealing, or if you hope to inhabit one of the harshest, totally barren deserts, one way to do it would be to build a self-contained habitation hidden underground, with a semi-closed recycling ecosystem built in. Or you might combine these two strategies and develop a permanent habitat, but look like a prospector when travelling away from home base.

The main factor to consider in planning a desert habitat is that no water would be continuously available from the environment. This fact at least offers the advantage that outsiders would not expect to find you living in a totally arid place. But life in even the driest desert is possible provided that you lived in an underground habitat that fully recycled water. The initial supply of water would have to be transported to the site. Or it might be gathered during an infrequent seasonal rainstorm. Then it would be stored in a man-made system that mimics the ability of cacti and other desert plants to store water in their tissues and to retard evaporation. Inside the habitat, water would be continually recycled with emphasis on minimizing losses from the system. Some losses will inevitably occur nevertheless, and makeup water will have to be brought in periodically from outside the area to top off the tanks. Or rain that falls no more than once a year might be an adequate source of makeup water.

Let's see how much rainwater would be available: A desert area usually receives ten inches or less of rain in a year. Ten inches of rain falling on a square 100 feet on a side, which has an area of 10,000 square feet, would total 8,333 cubic feet, which is over 62,000 gallons. This rainwater could be gathered by spreading a waterproof coating on an area that sloped to one corner in which a cistern would be placed. Such a 10,000 square foot catchment basin would gather 6,200 gallons of water for every inch of rain that falls on it. So it looks like it would be possible in most cases to obtain makeup water for a desert habitat from infrequent rain showers, provided the interval between showers is not too long.

Although most deserts have a season in which rain is more likely to fall, long periods may pass with no rain at all. The longest such rainless period on record is 35 months in the Mojave Desert in California, in a drought that ended in January 1920. But longer dry periods probably have occurred in other deserts where accurate records have not been kept. Adequate storage facilities would be needed to tide a desert dweller over such rainless periods. And in the worst case, water from outside would have to be brought in during an exceptionally long dry spell.

The first design consideration in a desert habitat is that drinking quality water shouldn't be unnecessarily contaminated. So the five gallon flush toilet is out of the question, and a waterless, composting toilet would be the preferred alternative. Lower quality water would be used where possible for purposes other than drinking. Thus, lightly contaminated water would be filtered and used for washing clothes and bodies, but not dishes. Urine could be added directly to a compost pile, or diluted with gray waste water and used to irrigate and fertilize food plants (grown inside). Gardens would be grown in a greenhouse that recaptures transpired moisture which would be recycled. Solar distillation of lower quality water under the desert sun would probably be the best method for producing top quality drinking water.

To prevent the loss of water and conditioned air, the underground desert habitat would be sealed airtight, so that air could only enter or leave as a result of deliberate ventilation. Entry to the habitat would be through an airlock. Placement underground would reduce the temperature variations that the habitat would be exposed to, would help to reduce air leaks, and would partially conceal it.

A couple other considerations are that the air would have to be kept at the optimum humidity and temperature by various means, including heavy reliance on ventilating with the right amounts of hot daytime air and cool night air. Although the air ventilation would be carefully controlled, there would be no need to attempt complete recycling of air. The desert sun appears to be by far the best energy source. Wind energy is also a possible source, but a wind generator is highly visible and would sacrifice concealment. Solar energy devices, on the other hand, can lie low near the ground, and can be made hard to find.

Plenty of food can be grown as long as water is provided. Where suitable soil is lacking, that would have to be imported -- or soilless hydroponics could be used. The gardens would have to be designed to minimize water loss, and for that reason gardens probably should be placed inside greenhouses for the most part. Small animals like chickens and rabbits could also be raised inside for their meat. If the outside desert environment is not totally hostile, it might make some contribution to the food supply, either through hunting and gathering, or by raising animals that are hardy and well-adapted to the local conditions and able to feed on native vegetation, or by growing plants suitable to the area with emphasis on minimizing the water required.

All deserts are under the sovereignty of some government or other, but some desolate, lightly populated areas are not very well controlled by the authorities. In such places a freedom seeker might manage to live unmolested. The following list shows the major desert areas of the world:

Kalahari	South Africa
Namib	Southwest Africa
Nefud	Northern Arabia
Rub 'al Khali (empty quarter)	Southern Arabia
Dhana	Arabia
Hamid	Arabia
Dasht-i-Kavir (salt desert)	Iran
Dasht-i-Lut	Iran
Kara Kum	Central Asia
Khorasan	Iran
Thar	Western India
Kizel Kum	Central Asia
Takla Makan	Western China
Gobi	Mongolia
Sind	Pakistan
Negev	Israel
Sinai	Egypt
Ghir Forest	India
Tarim Basin	Central Asia
Turfan Depression	Central Asia
Dzungaria	Central Asia
Gibsons	Australia
Great Sandy Desert	Australia
Simpson	Australia
Great Victoria	Australia
Death Valley	California
Monument Valley	Arizona
Great Salt Desert	Utah
White Sands	New Mexico
Chihuahua	Northern Mexico
Sonora	Northern Mexico
Mojave	California
Great Basin	Western North America
Atacama	Chile
Patagonia	Argentina
Sahara	North Africa

Finally, we have these last points to consider: A desert nomad would have all the living space he wants to use. But a modern desert troglodyte (underground dweller) would have to consider space more of a luxury since every cubic foot would have to be laboriously excavated. To make a living in the desert, location-independent sources of income look like the best option, unless one can find mineral resources that can be exploited.

With very little population and little industry, there is consequently not very much pollution in most deserts, though naturally occurring dust and blowing sand will often be prevalent. The desert nomadic lifestyle, while it is possible in some places, would be a rough way to live. But an underground habitat in the desert could be as comfortable as you want to make it, provided that you have enough money to spend in building and equipping it.

For more Information, see:

ALIVE IN THE DESERT, by Joe Kraus. Paladin Press, Boulder, Colorado, 1978. *Complete guide to desert recreation and survival. Includes information on water, shelter, food from plants and animals, the desert in winter, dangerous plants and animals, and much more.*

HOW TO CUT YOUR WATER USE IN HALF, by Randall Harrison. Communication Press, San Francisco, 1977. *Booklet giving tips on how to greatly reduce your use of water while still living in a conventional lifestyle.*

SUCCESSFUL GARDENING WITH LIMITED WATER, by Margaret Tipton Wheatley. Woodbridge Press, Santa Barbara, California, 1978. *This is a good place to start on the subject of growing while using a reduced amount of water, although this book covers only landscaping and flowering plants, rather than food plants.*

DUNE, by Frank Herbert. *A science fiction novel that depicts people living on a planet so dry that water is more precious than gold; so dry that people must wear "still-suits" to recapture every bit of their body's moisture.*

AFOOT IN THE DESERT. Desert Publications, Cornville, AZ 86325. *An Air Force manual for instructing downed fliers in desert survival.*

SUN, SAND, AND SURVIVAL. Desert Publications, Cornville, AZ 86325. *Stories of downed allied fliers who survived and walked out of the desert alive.*

DESERT OPERATIONS. Desert Publications, Cornville, AZ

86325. *A US Army manual giving instructions for military operations in the desert. It covers clothing, navigation, concealment, camouflage, preventive medicine, food, water, sleeping, physical conditioning, and much more.*

"Water Recycler Purifies Entire Household Supply", by Jane Kleintob, in POPULAR SCIENCE, June 1978. *Report on a device being sold by a company named PureCycle. It costs $5,000, is about the size of a car, and continuously recycles 500 gallons of water, using a biological process and a series of filters. For latest information, contact: PureCycle, 2855 Walnut Street, Boulder, CO 80301.*

PART V

1985 UPDATE

Chapter 1 - ANTARCTICA

• The civilian population of the Falkland Islands is now about 1800. Reports indicate that there is an acute shortage of young, unmarried women. Since the 1982 war, Britain has built up a large permanent garrison on these islands, which are expected to continue as a garrison state on into the indefinite future.

• The whaling station at Grytviken, South Georgia, was abandoned in 1964 and there is presently no permanent civilian population on the island. There is a British Antarctic research station on South Georgia, and, since the 1982 war in the South Atlantic, sometimes there is a British military presence in the area.

• In an attempt to grow vegetables in a greenhouse in Antarctica, New Zealand scientists set up a small, solar-heated greenhouse in the Taylor Valley area during the summer of 1970. Average temperatures of over 70°F, were maintained inside the greenhouse and beans and tomatoes were raised to the fruiting stage.

• A baby was born on January 7, 1978 at the Argentine Sargento Cabral Base in Antarctica. The infant, Emilio Marcos Palma, is the first person to have been born in Antarctica.

• ITT Antarctic Services, Inc. is the civilian contractor who provides support services for the US National Science Foundation research program in Antarctica. If you are not a scientist and would like to work in Antarctica, they are the people to contact about job openings. Write to them at 621 Industrial Ave., Paramus, NJ 07652.

• Several travel firms offer tourists a chance to visit Antarctica by ship, for a price in the range of $5000 to $8000 per person. **Lindblad Travel** sails to the ice in the "Lindblad Explorer," while **Society Expeditions** charters the "World Discoverer" for Antarctic voyages. For information about these voyages, see the article "Explorations" in the September 1982 issue of OMNI Magazine. Here are several addresses you can write to for information about these cruises:

Lindblad Travel, 8 Wright St., Westport, CT 06880
Society Expeditions, 723 Broadway East, Seattle, WA 98102
Special Expeditions, 133 East 55 St., New York, NY 10022
Sobek Expeditions, Angels Camp, CA 95222.

- ANTARCTICA: WILDERNESS AT RISK, by Barney Brewster, Friends of the Earth Books, San Francisco, 1982. *A conservationist warns that the imminent development of Antarctica poses a risk of pollution and destruction of wildlife. This is written by a New Zealander from a New Zealand perspective; full of details about Antarctic pollution, wildlife, resources, and exploitation prospects.*

- SURVIVAL IN ANTARCTICA, National Science Foundation, Washington, DC, 1979. *This 100 page government manual thoroughly covers the title subject including: clothing, shelters, overland travel, survival on sea ice, fire, and much more.*

- LIFE AT THE BOTTOM, The People of Antarctica, by John Langone; Little, Brown and Co., Boston, 1977. *Report of a journalist who spent a season in Antarctica focusing especially on the people who live and work there, including how they cope with such problems as boredom, cabin fever, and sexual deprivation.*

- LITTLE AMERICA, Town At The End Of The World, by Paul A. Carter, Columbia University Press, NY, 1979. *About the 5 Antarctic expeditions led by Richard E. Byrd which ushered in the successful use of machines in Antarctic exploration. On his first expedition in 1929, Byrd became the first person to fly over the South Pole. His team was also the first to establish 2-way radio communication from Antarctica.*

- ANTARCTIC LAW AND POLITICS, by F.M. Auburn, Hurst (Great Britain). *Explains how the political system based on the Antarctic Treaty works; covers territorial claims made by various nations, and control of wildlife and minerals, and environmental protection.*

- "Antarctica: Freeze-Dried Desert," by Charles Petit, in SCIENCE DIGEST, May 1981. *A striking photo-essay about Antarctica, includes information about the Ellsworth Mountains and the possibility of a collapse of the West Antarctic ice sheet which would raise ocean levels and drown coastal cities around the world.*

Chapter 2 - ARCTIC ICECAP

• The Arctic Ocean icepack is slowly melting away. During Nansen's drift on the "Fram" in the 1890's, the average thickness of the Arctic ice was measured at 12 feet. In 1937 to 1940 a Russian icebreaker, the "Sedov," drifted along a path similar to that followed by "Fram." The Russians found that the average thickness of the ice had shrunk to only 7 feet, a decline of 40% in 45 years. Also, the area covered by the Arctic icepack in summer is much smaller now than it was several decades ago. At the same time, northern shipping is encountering less sea ice, and northern ports are enjoying longer ice-free shipping months. Looking to the future, some scientists are predicting that in less than 100 years there may be no ice at all in the Arctic during summer months.

• Ice islands that drift in a circle on the North American side of the Arctic Ocean take 10 to 12 years to complete each circuit. Each time around they tend to veer farther to the outside of their circular course. The end may come when such an island veers to the left rather than the right as it approaches north Greenland. Then it will be caught in the East Greenland Current and carried toward the North Atlantic Ocean where it will melt. Or else it may turn right and swing by Greenland only to run aground somewhere among the Canadian Arctic islands where it will gradually melt away in summer. Ice islands have a lifespan of only about 30 years. But more continue to break off the Ellesmere Ice Shelf and will continue to do so for many years to come.

• THE WORLD OF ICE, by James L. Dyson, published by Alfred A. Knopf, NY, 1966. *All about glaciers, icebergs, icecaps, and sea ice, focusing especially on the Greenland Icecap and the Arctic Ocean icepack.*

Chapter 4 - SUB-ANTARCTIC ISLANDS

• UNINHABITED AND DESERTED ISLANDS, by Jon Fisher, ©1983, available for $7.95 plus $2 shipping from Loompanics Unltd., PO Box 1197, Port Townsend, WA 98368. *Includes longer, more complete descriptions of all the sub-Antarctic islands mentioned in this chapter.*

• ICE BIRD, The First Single-Handed Voyage to Antarctica, by David Lewis, W.W. Norton & Co., NY, 1975. *Lewis sailed alone from Australia, across the stormy far south Pacific to the Antarctic Peninsula area where he visited several islands. He spent some time at Palmer Base on Anvers Island, sailed up the Bransfield Strait and on to the South Orkney Islands where he stopped briefly at Signy Base, encountering an army of icebergs north of the Weddell Sea. Then he continued east and ended his voyage at Cape Town, South Africa.*

• ELEPHANT ISLAND, AN ANTARCTIC EXPEDITION, by Chris Furse, Anthony Nelson Ltd, Shropshire, England, 1979. *This is the story of the 1976 16-man British expedition which was the first to thoroughly explore and map Elephant Island and a few nearby smaller islands in the South Shetland Islands. Includes many detailed maps and photos. This expedition was the first to use ocean-going canoes in Antarctic exploration.*

Chapter 5 - FLOATING PLATFORM

• "Sea City," by Adam Starchild and James Holahan, in FUTURE LIFE #18, May 1980. *Describes a detailed proposal to build an artificial island-city at a shallow spot in the ocean (such shoal areas make up 10% of the world's oceans). Sea City would look like a huge amphitheater consisting of apartment and commercial blocks that rise like bleachers surrounding a lagoon. Details of construction, economic viability, food, drinking water, energy, amenities, etc. are all worked out.*

Chapter 6 - BOATS

• Here are 2 mail-order outfits that sell books about boats, ocean voyages, living aboard, etc. Write to them for their catalogs:

Seven Seas Press, 524 Thames St., Newport, RI 02840
International Marine Publishing Co., 21 Elm St., Camden, ME 04843.

• **SEVEN SEAS CRUISING ASSOCIATION BULLETIN** is now $18/year and they are at a new address: PO Box 2190, Covington, LA 70434.

• THE COMPLETE LIVE-ABOARD BOOK, by Katy Burke, ©1982, is available for $39.95 postpaid from Seven Seas Press, 524 Thames St., Newport, RI 02840. *This is a big 384 page book that tells you all you need to know to miniaturize your lifestyle down to complete floating mobility. Covers all the necessary details.*

Chapter 7 - DESERTED ISLANDS

• There are 2 US Government agencies that sell fine maps of many ocean islands. For information write to:

Defense Mapping Agency, Office of Distribution Services, Washington, DC 20315
US Department of Commerce, NOAA/NOS - C44, Riverdale, MD 20737.

• BLUEPRINT FOR PARADISE, How To Live On A Tropic Island, by Ross Norgrove, ©1983, International Marine Publishing Co., Camden, ME. *If you are ready to make your move to a tropical island, there are thousands of details to consider: How do you find the right island, buy property there, build a house? What about food, water, medical care, jobs, schools for your kids, etc? This book provides an authoritative discussion of all those details and more.*

• CASTAWAY, by Lucy Irvine, Random House, 1983. *Author Lucy Irvine describes the year (May 1981 to June 1982) that she spent with a fellow adventurer, a man she hardly knew, living isolated on a tiny, deserted island in the Torres Strait near Australia. This is a cautionary tale about what can go wrong if you move to a deserted island witho... ...per preparation,* written by one who has been there.

- A firm that specializes in selling private is... up, is Boehm and Vladi GmbH, Neuer Wall 2, for $20,000 on 36, West Germany. ...00, Hamburg

- Rare Earth Enterprises also sells islands, and ... publish a newsletter: RARE EARTH REPORT, 6 issues per ... r for $36. Write to Box 946-X, Sausalito, CA 94966.

- ISLANDS Magazine, 6 issues per year for $18, ... State St., Santa Barbara, CA 93105, *publishes articles a...ut rious islands, or that have some tie-in with islands, mostly ...out populated islands, but some tidbits about deserted island ...re mentioned.*

- UNINHABITED AND DESERTED ISLANDS, by Jon Fisher, ©1983, available for $7.95 plus $2 shipping from Loompanics Unltd., PO Box 1197, Port Townsend, WA 98368. *This is the updated and expanded second edition that incorporates the now out-of-print UNINHABITED PACIFIC ISLANDS; covers over 180 islands and groups of islands in the Atlantic, Pacific, Indian, and Antarctic Oceans; the only book in print that deals primarily with uninhabited islands.*

Chapter 8 - UNDERWATER HABITAT

- CONQUERING THE DEEP SEA FRONTIER, by Ray and Patricia Darby, David McKay Co., NY 1971. *Covers the pioneering underwater habitats of the 1960's, especially Tektite I and II and the Oceanic Foundation habitat known as Aegir.*

- "Here Comes Tektite III," by Mark E. Gibson, SKIN DIVER, February 1981. *When the very successful Tektite II US Government underwater research program ended, no one knew what to do with the habitat, so it sat around for a long time as so much surplus equipment. Finally, Dr. Hal Ross, who had become an enthusiast while on the Tektite II support team, formed a private organization, the Tektite Society, and they acquired the surplus habitat. It has now been refurbished and moved from the Virgin Islands to the Pacific Ocean off San*

d Tektite III, it will be used as a saturation
Fra*nc*isco. R*i*support of marine research and for diver
divi*ng* habit*...*
trai*n*ing.

- "The U*...* *D*eep: A New Frontier," by Stan Luxenberg, SCIENCE *...*EST, May 1981. *Covers the prospects, promises, and dang...faced b*y divers who work at depths gre*a*ter than 1000 fee*t. pres*sure chambers, divers have gone to simulated depth*s over *000 feet with no ill effects, while breathing care*... desi...ed gas mixtures. But remotely operat*ed mech-ani*c... devic*es are being used increasingly for really d*eep work.

- *...ider *he Sea, Locked in a pressure chamber, volunteers *...n up deep space*," by John F. Pearson, POPULAR MECH-*...ICS, *September 1981. Long, detailed article recounts the *p*roblems of diving below 1000 feet and the experiments with breathing gas mixtures that have enabled divers to set new simulated depth records of over 2000 feet.

- "The Deepest Dive," by Susan West, SCIENCE NEWS, March 21, 1981. Another report on the experiment that took divers down to a simulated record depth of 2250 feet.

- "Why Not Grow A Building Underwater," by David Lampe, NEXT, March 1980. A Texas professor has discovered a way to make structures from the minerals dissolved in seawater. He fabricates wire mesh into the desired shape and runs a small DC electric current thru it while it's submerged in seawater. A mineral deposit containing magnesium and calcium electro-plates onto the mesh and fills in the spaces, forming a solid structure. With this technique an underwater habitat, or an entire artificial island, could be grown in place and would require importing only a minimum of building materials.

- "Unlimited Underwater Activity Made Possible By Invention of Hemosponge." Hemosponge is something like artificial fish gills, a plastic material that can extract oxygen from seawater. It's use would enable divers to breath underwater the way fish do without carrying a limited air supply. For more information write to Don Seaver, Duke University, 615 Chapel Drive, Durham, NC 27706. From LEADING EDGE, PO Box 42247, Los Angeles, CA 90042.

Chapter 9 - SUBMARINE

• "Submersibles, Exploring the earth's last, deepest frontier," by Anthony Wolff, OMNI, July 1981. *Photo-essay showing the lastest developments in submarine workboats and habitats.*

• "The Descent of Man," by Sylvia Earle, SCIENCE 81, September 1981, *Recent advances in diving systems are pushing the practical depth limit where real work can be done from the present 2000 foot level to 5000 feet, opening new areas to petroleum engineers and seabed miners.*

• **Sub Schools Inc.,** 2915 Saxon Drive, Midland, MI 48640. Offers instruction in operation and handling of the modified Kittredge K-250 submarine, and builds custom-made subs to order.

• The US Navy held hearings in Olympia, Washington in February 1983 concerning a proposal to dispose of the 100 nuclear submarines that will become obsolete in the next 30 years by scuttling them off the coast of northern Calilfornia. Five nuclear submarines have already been decommissioned and are awaiting disposal. (from SEATTLE TIMES, February 20, 1983)

Chapter 10 - WALKING NOMAD

• WALKING JOURNAL, quarterly magazine, $8.00 per year, from PO Box 454, Athens, GA 30603.

• NOMADIC BOOKS, newsletter and catalog, PO Box 454, Athens, GA 30603, *sells books about cheap, independent, and concerned traveling. They'll send you a catalog for a 20¢ stamp.*

• VAGABONDING IN THE USA, by Ed Buryn. This is the new edition of VAGABONDING IN AMERICA, 432 pages, ©1983, $12.00 postpaid from PO Box 31123, San Francisco, CA 94131. *Covers unusual strategies and techniques for traveling cheaply and independently throughout America.*

• LAND NAVIGATION, by W.S. Kals, $10.70 postpaid from Sierra Club Books, 530 Bush St., San Francisco, CA 94108, 230 pages, ©1983. *Very clear instruction in how to find your way on the trail or traveling cross-country, including map reading, navigating by the stars, using a compass and an altimeter.*

• You can get great maps by mail from Eagle Eye Graphics, PO Box 30917, Seattle, WA 98103. Write for their free catalog of Traveler's Maps.

• RANDOM HOUSE GUIDE TO NATURAL AREAS OF THE EASTERN US, by John Perry and Jane Greverus Perry, 835 pages, ©1980, $12.95 postpaid from Random House, 400 Hahn Road, Westminster, MD 21157. *This big book describes nature preserves, parks, and undeveloped areas all up and down the East Coast.*

Chapter 11 - BICYCLE NOMAD

• THE ALL NEW COMPLETE BOOK OF BICYCLING, by Eugene A. Sloane, 736 pages, ©1981, $20.70 postpaid from Simon and Schuster, Attn: Mail Order, 1230 Avenue of the Americas, New York, NY 10020. *This may be the best bicycle repair book, with very clear, well-illustrated repair instructions. It covers almost everything that may affect a bike and rider. The author speaks from extensive bicycling experience.*

• THE BICYCLING BOOK, by John Krausz and Vera van der Reis Krausz, 280 pages, ©1982, $11.95 postpaid from Dial Press, Doubleday and Co., 501 Franklin Ave., Garden City, NY 11530. *A collection of bicycling advice and information from several authorities, covers a variety of bike topics, not another bike repair book. It includes sections on equipment, clothing, riding safety, recreational cycling, and more.*

• HUMAN POWER, newsletter of the International Human Powered Vehicle Association, 4 issues per year for $15.00. *Reports on innovative developments concerning vehicles solely powered by people.* IHPVA, PO BOX 2068, Seal Beach, CA 90740.

• BICYCLING THE PACIFIC COAST, by Tom Kirkendall and Vicky Spring, 224 pages, ©1984, $8.95 postpaid from The Mountaineers, 715 Pine St., Seattle, WA 98101. *This is a guidebook to the 2000 mile bicycle route that has been laid out along the US West Coast from Canada to Mexico, with cheap campsites within a day's ride of each other. You can use it to plan your trip.*

Chapter 12 - CANOE NOMAD

• Building your own canoe is quite feasible. To find out how, send for the free catalog from Outdoor Sports, PO Box 1213, Tuscaloosa, AL 35401, which lists plans for building canoes, kayaks, and other small boats, and books about canoeing.

• **American Canoe Association**, Book Service, PO Box 248, Lorton, VA 22079. Upon request, they'll send you a list describing the books that they sell about canoeing.

• DOWN RIVER MAGAZINE, 6 issues per year for $4.00, PO Box 366, Mountain View, CA 94040.

• CANOEING MAGAZINE, 12 issues per year for $10.50. 25 Featherbed Lane, Croydon, CRO 9AE, England.

• CANOE, the magazine of self propelled water travel, 6 issues per year for $15.00, PO Box 10748, Des Moines, IA 50349.

• THE COMPLETE WILDERNESS PADDLER, by James West Davidson and John Rugge, $5.95 postpaid, order no. 71153-X, from Random House Mail Service, Dept. C-CWP 11-2, 201 East 50th St., New York, NY 10022. *Covers the planning, outfitting, and conducting of both still and whitewater canoe trips.*

Chapter 13 - HORSE NOMAD

• THINK HARMONY WITH HORSES, by Ray Hunt, 87 pages, ©1978, $14.45 postpaid from Give-It-A-Go Enterprises, PO Box 28, Tuscarora, NV 89834. *The author is an experienced horseman who holds clinics on handling horses around the country. This book is edited from tapes of several of those sessions. Contains the condensed wisdom of a hands-on-expert.*

• A source of traditional, rugged camp equipment, including tack for pack horses, heavy canvas tents, camp stoves, etc., is Beckel Camp Products, 2232 SE Clinton, Portland, OR 97202.

• PACKIN' IN (ON MULES AND HORSES), by Smoke Elser and Bill Brown, 158 pages, ©1980, $9.95 postpaid from Mountain Press, PO Box 2399, Missoula, MT 59806. *This is a book by packers with years of experience who tell how to pack in anything up to and including a piano; also covers selecting equipment and animals, leading a string of pack animals, and lots of tips on camping.*

- TECHNIQUES AND EQUIPMENT FOR WILDERNESS HORSE TRAVEL, 42 pages, ©1981, USDA Forest Service booklet, free from Missoula Equipment Development Center, Building One, Ft. Missoula, Missoula, MT 59801. *Sketchy, but contains useful plans for homemade gear, and valuable horse camping tips. Anyway, the price is right.*

Chapter 15 - CAMPER

- "King of the Road, Living with Technology," by Julia Homer, in TECHNOLOGY ILLUSTRATED, November 1983, *is about the luxurious, high-cost end of camper life, how to do it if you're rich, in a $300,000 converted "Greyhound"-type bus.*

- HOME IS WHERE YOU PARK IT, by Kay Peterson. The second edition is now available, 221 pages, ©1982, $8.95 postpaid from Roving Press, c/o Peterson, PO Box 2870, MCCA, Estes Park, CO 80517.

- ESCAPEES (A Newsletter For Full-Time Rovers), is for people whose "recreational vehicle" is their only home, 6 issues per year for $20.00, from Roving Press, c/o Peterson, PO Box 2870, MCCA, Estes Park, CO 80517.

- MCCA Worldwide Mail Forwarding Service, gives you an address to which your mail can be sent if you move around a lot, and will forward your mail to you. Costs about $45 per year. For free information, write to MCCA, PO Box 2870, Estes Park, CO 80517.

- CARBOOK, 181 Glen Ave., Sea Cliff, NY 11579, sells shop manuals and other books about cars and other vehicles, including several books about vans and campers. Send $1.00 for their catalog.

- VONU, THE SEARCH FOR PERSONAL FREEDOM, by Rayo, edited by Jon Fisher, ©1983, available for $5.95 plus $2 shipping from Loompanics Unltd, PO Box 1197, Port Townsend, WA 98368. *Collected in this book are the writings of Rayo, who took* to living as a van nomad to enhance his own freedom. You can learn from the words of one who actually lived this way just how it's done and the rationale behind it.

Chapter 16 - AIRSHIPS

• AIRSHIP SAGA, "The history of airships seen through the eyes of the men who designed, built, and few them," by Lord Ventry and Eugene M. Kolesnik, 192 pages, ©1982, Blandford Books Ltd., distributed in US by Sterling Publishing Co., 2 Park Ave, New York, NY 10016.

• "Publicity Boost for Airships," in NEW SCIENTIST, August 23, 1984, mentions that a British airship, "Skyship 500," is being evaluated for possible future use by the US Coast Guard and the US Navy.

• THE AIRSHIP: DODO OR PHOENIX, by Robert W. Lockesby, 12 pages, March 1981, lists 145 references, mostly books and magazine articles, relating to airships. You can get a copy for $2.00 from Vance Bibliographies, PO Box 229, Monticello, IL 61856. Ask for Public Administration Series: Bibliographies No. P-693.

• "Now We're Ballooning on Solar Power," by M. Storey Smith, in POPULAR MECHANICS, April 1982, describes a hot air balloon that uses solar energy for part of its lift. This double envelope balloon has been flown across the English Channel.

• "Airships Come Of Age," by Marv Wolf, in SOLDIER OF FORTUNE, April 1981. This is a very detailed article that tells you all about the Goodyear Blimps, the most important airships flying today, with short sidebars about other related airship topics.

• "A Better Blimp," item in the "Continuum" column in OMNI, September 1982. Describes a revolutionary new airship design consisting of a rotating, helium-filled sphere with a fuselage hanging down below it. A 20 foot diameter prototype has been built and flown, and a 180 foot diameter full-sized version is planned.

• "Once-Mighty Blimps Flying High Again, soaring fuel costs, decaying roads/rails breathe life into airships," by Kevin Anderson, USA TODAY, December 30, 1982.

• "Born-Again Blimps," by Mae Rudolph, SCIENCE DIGEST, June 1981. *Futuristic speculation about possible airship designs that might be built, including a "helium horse" bulk cargo carrier, luxury passenger airliners with spacious dancefloors and promenade decks, "heavy lifter" helicopter/airship hybrid, and nuclear-powered airships.*

Chapter 19 - CAVERNS

• DISCOVERY AT THE RIO CAMUY, by Russell and Jeane Gurnee, 181 pages, ©1973, Crown Publishers Inc., 419 Park Ave. South, New York, NY 10016. *Tells about how one of the largest caves in Puerto Rico was found and explored during several expeditions over many years. Gives the reader a clear general impression of the conditions inside this type of underground river cavern.*

• UNDERGROUND SPACE: A NEW RESOURCE, by Christine E. Moe, 12 pages, July 1981, *is a list of 140 references concerned with building and using underground space.*You can get a copy for $2.00 from Vance Bibliographies, PO Box 229, Monticello, IL 61856. Ask for Public Administration Series: Bibliography No. P-768.

Chapter 20 - DESERTS

DESERT HARVEST, A Guide To Vegetable Gardening in Arid Lands, by Jane Nyhuis, 63 pages, ©1982, $7.00 postpaid from Meals For Millions, PO Box 42622, Tucson, AZ 85733. *This beginner's guide to organic vegetable gardening in desert conditions such as one finds in southern Arizona, describes techniques and recommends appropriate vegetable varieties.*

YOU WILL ALSO WANT TO READ:

CONTROVERSIAL AND UNUSUAL BOOKS!!!

"Yes, there are books about the skills of apocalypse -- spying, surveillance, fraud, wire-tapping, smuggling, self-defense, lockpicking, gunmanship, eavesdropping, car chasing, civil warfare, surviving jail, and dropping out of sight. Apparently writing books is the way mercenaries bring in spare cash between wars. The books are useful, and it's good the information is freely available (and they definitely inspire interesting dreams), but their advice should be taken with a salt shaker or two and all your wits. A few of these volumes are truly scary. Loompanics is the best of the Libertarian suppliers who carry them. Though full of 'you'll-wish-you'd-read-these-when-it's-too-late' rhetoric, their catalog is genuinely informative."
-THE NEXT WHOLE EARTH CATALOG

Now available:
THE BEST BOOK CATALOG IN THE WORLD!!!

- *Large 8½ x 11 size!*
- *More than 500 of the most controversial and unusual books ever printed!!!*
- *YOU can order EVERY book listed!!!*
- *Periodic Supplements to keep you posted on the LATEST titles available!!!*

We offer hard-to-find books on the world's most unusual subjects. Here are a few of the topics covered IN DEPTH in our exciting new catalog:

- *Hiding/concealment of physical objects! A complete section of the books ever written on hiding things!*
- *Fake ID/Alternate Identities! The most comprehensive selection of books on this little-known subject ever offered for sale! You have to it to believe it!*
- *Investigative/Undercover methods and techniques! Professional secrets known only to a few, now revealed for YOU to use! Actual police manuals on shadowing and surveillance!*
- *And much, much more, including Locks and Locksmithing, Self Defense, Intelligence Increase, Life Extension, Money-Making Opportunities, and much, much more!*

Our book catalog is truly THE BEST BOOK CATALOG IN THE WORLD! Order yours today -- you will be very pleased, we know.

(Our catalog is free with the order of any book on the previous page -- or is $2.00 if ordered by itself.)

Loompanics Unlimited
PO Box 1197
Pt Townsend, WA 98368
USA